LIFE'S LITTLE LESSONS

NANCY LEE BEAVERS

Corrine –
You will never have
know the impact you have
made on my life through the
"Years". Your beautiful Spirit
is glowing.
Love You,
Nancy

DEDICATION

I dedicate this book to my precious
Mother, Willie Juanita Mills.
My role model – a woman of great faith.
One of her dreams was to write a book -
a dream fulfilled through her daughter.

With Love,
Nancy Lee

CONTENTS

ACKNOWLEDGEMENTS

To my wonderful, supportive husband Gary - who has been there in good and bad times sharing these LESSONS I have learned. His knowledge in technology has helped me make this book possible.

To my precious son and daughter, Darren and Dawn who have brought me years of happiness in the blessed "profession of Motherhood."

To my six awesome grandchildren;   Erailia, Rachel, Samantha, Payton, Karissa and Jaida. You light up my life!

To my loving Christian parents who introduced me to the Lord many years ago.

To my extended family (which are many) who has shared in love, tears and laughter through the years.

To my Special JOYTIME buddies; Janette, Patricia, and Sharon, who have shared many years of laughter and tears.

To all of my FRIENDS from church, work, and everyday life.

To Patricia Conaway and Becca Jackson for their encouragement to finish my book.

To Roxy Wiley and Donna Britton for editing the manuscript.

To Cindy Miller for proofreading the book.

Last, but MOST IMPORTANT, to JESUS CHRIST, MY LORD the one who teaches me LIFE'S LITTLE LESSONS.

FOREWORD

Nan,

What a lovely treasure you have created for all who love and cherish you! I so enjoyed your journey through the years and how God remained your constant focus.

Thanks for letting me read and edit it. I had a fun time!

Love,

Roxy

Roxy Wiley
Director of Women's Ministry
Liberty Bible Church

LIFE'S LITTLE LESSONS

Preface

One of my dreams and goals since I was in my early twenties has been to write a book. I started this book at age forty-two. I have put it aside, not intentionally, but life has happened. Since I am now sixty-five, I believe one of the encouraging factors I have realized is I'm not getting any younger, but I'm getting wiser. (Well, that's my way of saying older - it sounds better!). Really, with a son Darren Ward, age forty-four, and a daughter Dawn Lee, age forty, and six grandchildren, I have been experiencing that old sentimental, nostalgic feeling - my babies have gone through their childhood, those wonderful teen years, and now they are adults. My husband Gary and I are now retired and spending a lot of time together ALONE. It's harder to keep my hair color "naturally" brunette. Time is slipping away very quickly!

I started writing in 1991 on my summer break as an elementary school secretary. One of my "Big" projects, after that infamous task of putting together a senior's graduation open house, was to put all of those "loose" snapshots (thrown in my bottom desk drawer and not in photo albums) organized and in their rightful place.

My two day walk down memory lane, finding poems I had written through the years, and an encouraging word from one of my special Joytime friends, Patricia, (while sharing a relaxing summer day at the beach) sparked enthusiasm to write my book - "It's Now or Never"!

Let's begin at the beginning.

INTRODUCTION

I have found out there are many lessons you can learn just "living" every day to its fullest. This is a book to share some little lessons I have learned through the years. It's personal, but that's how I've learned these lessons - with Jesus Christ as my personal Savior. He has given me glimpses of Joy, Patience, Hope, Faith, Peace, triumph through trials, and has been and will always be my CONSTANT friend while learning LIFE'S LITTLE LESSONS.

THEME VERSE:

I CAN DO ALL THINGS THROUGH CHRIST WHO STRENGTHENETH ME.
Philippians 4:13 (KJV)

LESSON 1

LIFE'S BEGINNING IS IMPORTANT

FOR GOD SO LOVED THE WORLD THAT HE GAVE HIS ONLY BEGOTTEN SON, THAT WHOSOEVER BELIEVETH IN HIM, SHOULD NOT PERISH, BUT HAVE EVERLASTING LIFE.   JOHN 3:16 (KJV)

On October 4, 1948, life began for me. I really don't remember that day, but it all happened in a hospital in Paducah, Kentucky.

My mother, father and a brother Jim, eight years old at the time, welcomed me into the world. Let me tell you right now - James Charles Mills and Willie Juanita (Yates) Mills - known as Juanita, Nita or fondly called Baby by my dad, were and are to this day the most precious parents any child could ever hope and dream of having. A lot of "kids" will tell you they have the BEST parents in the world - well mine are the BEST! But, of course, when you're told you are just what they ordered, you have to think they're really special! They are so special I could write a book all about them and their sixty-five years of married life and service for the Lord, so they'll be mentioned many times throughout my lessons of life, because they truly taught me many.

Being a "preacher's kid" made life's beginning exciting, challenging, believe it or not, never boring. Some would say being at the church an hour early every time the doors were opened and being active in all phases of the church as a child would be boring, but that was my life and it was not boring! There were many decisions to make throughout my childhood - like all children's lives, but the first lesson I learned at an early age was to talk things over with the Lord before I came to a decision.

I came to know my special friend "Jesus Christ" at age seven at an evening service at our church. The speaker talked of accepting Jesus as your "personal" Savior. Mom and Dad had already shared this wonderful Jesus in our home and

I was ready to ask Him into my heart. I had memorized the familiar words " For God so loved the world that He gave His only begotten son, that whosoever believeth in Him should not perish but have everlasting life." John 3:16 (KJV). Everlasting! Wow! That's FOREVER! At first I hesitated about making my decision public that night because my Daddy was not there to see me walk down the aisle. He was preaching at an evangelistic meeting at another church. I thought I should wait until he could be there. But, that first basic lesson of talking to the Lord before making any decisions started right then and there. It was a feeling or an urging to let me know my "Heavenly Daddy" was knocking at my heart's door and my wonderful earthly Daddy would understand and know how important it was to answer that call that very night.

So life's beginning is important - not only for physical life, but for spiritual life. To know Jesus lived and died for me, and most of all that He lives today, makes life worth living.

LESSON 2

HOW TO SURVIVE THOSE IN-BETWEEN YEARS

GO YE, THEREFORE, AND TEACH ALL NATIONS, BAPTIZING THEM IN THE NAME OF THE FATHER, AND OF THE SON, AND OF THE HOLY SPIRIT. TEACHING THEM TO OBSERVE ALL THINGS WHATSOEVER I HAVE COMMANDED YOU; AND LO I AM WITH YOU ALWAYS, EVEN UNTO THE END OF THE WORLD. MATTHEW 28:19-20. (KJV)

It's kind of hard to think back and tell about my teen years. They were my in-between time. I was too old for Barbies and too young to date. With my brother being eight years older than I, we never had those brother - sister knock-down-drag-out fights. The only argument I can remember is who was going to lick the applesauce cake bowl, (mom's famous recipe), and that was only in fun! Jim was already married and in the Navy. I finally had the sister I always wanted in his sweet wife, Janette. She was the one who taught me how to wear make-up and all those etiquette rules clumsy teenage girls need to learn. I guess you could say, during my in-between days, I was like an only child.

I also had the challenge of "being in a fish bowl" with many looking at me as a teenage preacher's kid. (P.K.) Like the movie, "I Was a Teenage Werewolf", I Was a Teenage P.K.! I can remember trying very hard to live for the Lord by continuing to stay active in church and being a good witness to my non-Christian friends at school.

I wanted to be accepted like all teens. Some teenagers try dressing like their friends and being in-style. The sixties craze meant wearing flip-up hair styles, white lipstick, and guys' rings with pastel angora wrapped around them. I went along with the styles and even attended parties, proms, and the hang-out in town. But my lesson to survive the teen years was Beware of Compromising. I praise the Lord that I never smoked a cigarette or drank alcohol. It was only through HIS strength, not mine!

It's hard to say, "NO", sometimes when tempted to go along with the crowd and not to give into feelings, especially if you think you love someone. But, even back then, the verse found in Philippians 4:13, "I can do all things through Christ who strengthens me", brought me through some temptations which could have jeopardized my life's dreams, goals, and the Lord's plan for my life.

I was very active in our mission organization, Girl's Auxiliary (later called Acteens). I had a very strong interest and love for missionary work. I loved to study about missionaries and how they shared Jesus Christ wherever they were. I decided at a summer G.A. Camp at age 13, while sitting on my favorite log during morning devotions, that I wanted to become a missionary. Matthew 28:19-20 was a verse that led me to my decision. "Go ye therefore and teach all nations, baptizing them in the name of the Father and the Son, and of the Holy Spirit. Teaching them to observe all things whatsoever I have commanded you; and lo, I am with you always, even unto the end of the world." As I sat on that log in God's beautiful creation, I read the words to our theme song for the week as a prayer and commitment.

HIS WAY MINE

GOD HAS A PLACE FOR EVERY PLANNED CREATION
A PATH FOR EVERY STAR TO GO.
HE DREW THE COURSE FOR EVERY RIVERS JOURNEY
NOW I KNOW HE HAS A WAY FOR ME.

I PLACE MY LIFE IN THE HANDS OF GOD
THOSE HANDS SO SCARRED NOW OUTSTRETCHED FOR ME
WHEREVER IT MAY BE - OVERLAND, OVERSEA
MAY THY WILL SUBLIME - OH THOU GOD DIVINE
BE MINE!

The memories of my eight years at summer camp are so special because my mother was there with me. She also had a strong desire to share in God's missionary work. Because of mother's guidance and the encouragement of our State Woman's Missionary Union Director, Louise Berge Winningham, I learned to be disciplined and to memorize scripture and to serve the Lord. My love for Missions grew even stronger.

LESSON 3

SOMETIMES THERE ARE CURVES AND DETOURS IN LIFE'S ROAD

I SOUGHT THE LORD, AND HE HEARD ME, AND DELIVERED ME FROM ALL MY FEARS. PSALMS 34:4 (KJV)

All through my high school years, well even during my elementary and junior high years, I loved to sing and play the piano. I played the piano for church services and activities, and I also loved to sing solos. I felt music would be a big part in my missionary calling. I had those infamous piano lessons. Practice, practice, practice! My favorite time to practice was after dinner when it was time for the dishes to be done. Mom always let practicing win over dishes. Of course, today whenever I'm visiting my mother, I always do her dishes-to try to make up for the guilt of getting out of them as a child.

I'll never forget the anxious feelings I had. It seemed like my first major crisis, another opportunity to ask the Lord, "NOW" what do I do? What does this mean? Why did this happen?"

We moved to a new town when I was a sophomore in high school. Dad had felt God called him to a new ministry in the area, and after two years of driving thirty miles many times a week for church activities, we decided we needed to move closer to the church. At first I didn't know how this would affect my life. Would the teens there accept a "new kid on the block"- especially a P.K.? But everything went real well. I met new friends and became active in the high school music department. Then one day I had a real sore throat, just a cold I thought. It seemed harder and harder to talk. (Which never seemed hard to me before!) Within a couple of weeks my singing was affected, and I had to go to a throat specialist. He ordered me not to talk for three weeks. OH NO! A female not talking for three whole weeks! Doctors said that my throat needed complete rest until they could find the problem. Can you believe that? I'd only been at the school one year. I had lots of new friends, I was getting asked to sing solos, and the

6

kids didn't look at me like I had a disease because I was a P.K. (Well some of them). I wore a sign, "I'm not stuck up- I just can't talk!" Plus, I carried a bell to get people's attention, and a paper and pencil to communicate at all times. Oh Lord, what next? Yep, you guessed it, surgery! X-rays and tests (You know, that real long scope with a light they put down your throat and it feels like it's reaching your toes,) was done. The doctors said I had a nodule or singer's node on my vocal cords and it needed to be removed.

The hospital stay went O.K. (Well, after they moved me off of the pediatric floor from a room of crying two through ten year olds to a "big" girls' room). I learned another lesson in humility!

My throat healed pretty well for talking, but singing came slowly. I can remember our new choral directors' face upon her arrival when I was introduced as Nancy Mills, the vice-president of the choir who couldn't sing! Miss Sandra Martz wondered what kind of choir it was! But it gave me an opportunity to "live" on the piano bench the remainder of my high school career. Music was a real joy in my life.

LESSON 4

OUR TIMING IS NOT ALWAYS GOD'S TIMING
COULD IT BE LOVE?

WAIT ON THE LORD; BE OF GOOD COURAGE, AND HE SHALL STRENGTHEN THINE HEART. WAIT I SAY ON THE LORD. PSALMS 27:14 (KJV)

My sixteenth birthday party was a blast! Mom and Dad rented the town skating rink and we invited my church and school friends for an exciting evening of skating and celebration. I was and had been interested in a boy from our past church for several years. He seemed pretty special to me. He was a Christian and that was the major asset. As my party went along, my friend Dennis Beavers' older brother "crashed" the celebration. (Well, came uninvited to check things out.) He happened to be dating one of my girlfriends. My first impression was not great. He was "real cute", but my heart belonged to another - so I thought! I ended up skating with Gary Beavers the rest of the night. (I don't recommend skating with your girlfriend's boyfriend all evening as a way to help your friendships along.) By the end of the evening, I was swept off my feet, and not because of falling down doing the Hokey-Pokey!

Well, the guy I told you about earlier was away at college and unexpectedly came home. I had a decision to make. He wanted me to go Christmas shopping and Gary had asked me out! Oh no! I wondered what I should do. I had a deep feeling - as deep as you can get for knowing someone two months - that Gary was the one for me.

Gary and I started seeing each other some, plus he started coming to our church. What more could I want? The most important thing was for Gary to become a Christian. I knew that a Christian mate for my future was in God's plan. Of course, I couldn't begin to think of that then - I had to get ready for missionary work. But wait, through prayer and my father's counseling, Gary was won to the Lord. Hallelujah! I thought I had my missionary husband for the future! I know

8

this sounds rushed for a junior in high school, but I'm telling it like it was!

After Gary's conversion, we thought Bible College would be great for him. His dream was to be a youth director. Wow Lord! Do you need youth directors in Africa? I was really excited about all of these plans. Gary went off to school in Kentucky. I planned to go after graduation. I was still four hundred miles away in Indiana finishing my senior year. We kept the mailman hopping with letters from each other. But absence did make our hearts grow fonder. And then to top it off, after I graduated from high school, I went to Kentucky to school and Gary stayed in Indiana. Now, this just wasn't working out. How could we ever be missionaries together in Africa if we couldn't even get together in one state at the same time?

However, the plan was unfolding. Gary came to Kentucky at the end of my freshman year of college and while on a riverboat ride presented me with a beautiful diamond ring, asking the question, " Will you marry me?" Of course, I said , "YES!" Even though I wanted to finish college, I most wanted to become Mrs. Gary Ward Beavers. Little did I know my father had already picked out a yellow Mustang convertible for me to take back to school my sophomore year. Gary teases him to this day by saying, "We should have at least waited until she got the car!"

Plans were in the making for an August 12, 1967, wedding. How exciting! My girlfriends Lana, Debbie, and Kathy were to be my attendants. They were all going to be dressed in yellow - my favorite color. After many trips for fittings and final touches the wedding was all set. Our family and friends gave me three bridal showers, announcements were out, and dum-dum-de-dum, we were on our way! Or were we?

"No, Lord, not another detour in my life!" Plan A was to be a missionary. (I still had hope). Plan B was to marry Gary Beavers, my dream guy, and the one I knew God had picked out for me.   Three weeks before the wedding, Gary called it off. "Cold feet", he said. The guys at work had been teasing him about getting "tied down". His best friend was going through a divorce. Why did that affect us? My mind raced after the tears were shed. What should I do with all of those gifts from three showers? What would people say? How could we contact three hundred people to tell them the wedding was off? Everything was all set, down to the napkins engraved with the words Nancy and Gary, August 12th, 1967. (My parents used the napkins the whole following year.)

I returned the beautiful diamond ring, hoped my girlfriends had use for their long yellow dresses, and tried to give this "BIG ONE" to the Lord. After all, it was the second biggest decision in my life. The first one was accepting my special friend Jesus. This time, it was almost too hard to give my problem to the Lord. Plan B had failed!

Mom and Dad decided to take me on a three week vacation. We would go to Florida to visit my grandparents, and visit Washington D.C. and all of the wonderful sights there. My parents thought the trip and the time away would help me pull myself together and get ready to return to college in January to continue my education. The only problem was, they strongly suggested I not even write Gary a postcard, make no phone calls to him, make no contact at all. Their advice was to just try to wait and see what the Lord had planned for me without him. Gary's mother Audrey ,whom I now call "Ma" said, " I wouldn't marry him if he was the last person on this earth." Now wait a minute, his own mother said that? Why couldn't I get him off my mind? Out of my heart?

When we returned home from our vacation, I decided maybe the best thing to do to forget Gary Beavers was to start dating other guys. After all, "There's more than one fish in the sea" , I was told. Word had gotten out I was no longer engaged, so I did have some phone calls and invitations for dates. My first date with someone else did not start out very well. After we left my house, we went a few blocks to a stop sign, and who was at the corner but Gary and a girl. ANOTHER GIRL! Now this part really sounds strange, but it happened, and I might as well share it to let you know "love affects you in many ways!" It even makes you sick!

When I dated others, I would throw up! (That's the best way I can put it). I developed a nervous stomach and every time I was with another guy I'd think of Gary because I still loved him so much. That in turn made my stomach upset and then you know what would happen. (I'll try not to use the term too often, in case you are a reader with a weak stomach.) After a month's time and several dates with others, Gary started getting jealous.

Oh boy, that's what I wanted. But not to the point of him following my dates home. (Later, I found out that was what he was doing.) We even tried to go out with each other once or twice, but I got sick then also. "What is going on?" I asked the Lord. This guy was tearing me apart! I started dating one of my friends pretty steadily. But, I knew he was not a Christian. And as I said before, that was my number one qualification in a future husband.

I learned at an early age not to pray for patience. Patience comes from testing and trials. "Count it all joy when you fall into various trials. Knowing this, that the testing of your faith worketh patience." James 1:2-3. So, I was praying to understand God's plan for my life. I wondered if it would ever include Gary Beavers again? I continued dating, but all the time I was praying and waiting for Gary to come back. I thought next time he should come on his knees. HE DID! And, "on his knees", he asked me once again to be his bride.

On January 13, 1968, (we didn't waste any time after the final decision) we had a beautiful winter wedding. Naturally, the girls could not wear yellow in a January snowstorm, and the only dresses we could get at a short notice were avocado green. I couldn't stand the color green, but it really didn't matter at that point! The wedding was really special, especially since my brother Jim walked me down the aisle, and my father performed the ceremony. Dad made it through, (oh he did forget one of the solos), without a tear until the song, "The Lord's Prayer", was sung. There wasn't a dry eye in the church, especially when I reached up and kissed my father before we marched down the aisle as Mr. and Mrs. Gary Ward Beavers. Daddy's little girl had been given away to a wonderful Christian man, but Dad would always have a special place in my heart.

DAD
THERE'S A SPECIAL MAN IN MY LIFE
FOR THAT I'M VERY GLAD.
HE'S BEEN THERE SINCE THE DAY I WAS BORN
THAT SPECIAL ONE IS MY DAD.

HIS LOVE MEANS SO MUCH TO ME
WHEN I NEEDED HIM - HE WAS ALWAYS THERE
HE'D GIVE TILL HE COULD GIVE NO MORE
FOR HE'S ALWAYS LOVED TO SHARE.

THE MEMORIES OF TIME GONE BY
ARE ALL HAPPY, JOYFUL AND GAY.
WHAT'S SO WONDERFUL ABOUT IT THOUGH
I FEEL THE SAME WHEN I'M WITH HIM TODAY.

HIS LOVE FOR US I'VE BEEN TELLING
BUT MORE IMPORTANT IS HIS LOVE FOR GOD
FOR IN DAD'S LIFE I CAN SEE HIM
EVERY FOOTSTEP HE HAS TROD.

HE'S REALLY A WALKING MIRACLE
SINCE GOD HAS SPARED HIS LIFE,
BUT YOU KNOW GOD HAS A HELPER
AND THIS HELPER IS DAD'S WIFE!

I COULD GO ON FOREVER
AND TELL WHAT THIS MAN MEANS TO ME,
BUT ON THIS SPECIAL FATHER'S DAY
I'M JUST SO HAPPY, THIS MAN I COULD SEE!

Written by Nancy Lee
For my Dad
Father's Day, 1974

LESSON 5

YOU CAN ORDER YOUR CHILDREN

CALL UNTO ME, AND I WILL ANSWER THEE, AND SHOW
THEE GREAT AND MIGHTY THINGS, WHICH THOU
KNOWEST NOT. JEREMIAH 33:3 (KJV)

Life as Mr. and Mrs. Beavers was true happiness.
Now, I will not say it was perfect. It required getting adjusted
to trivial everyday habits such as one of us squeezing the
toothpaste tube in the middle, and the other rolling it up from
the bottom (I won't tell which one did which), and not coming
to eat dinner on the first, second or third call. Oh, I can
remember one evening "crying" over that one! We lived in the
country in a little rented farm house. Gary was very busy
shooting his shotgun out in the backyard. (You could do that
where we lived.) I called him to come eat the gourmet dinner
I had cooked as a young bride with not a lot of cooking
experience. I called again and again. Finally, the tears came
as I called one more time adding, "Dinner is getting cold!" He
finally came and sat down to a bacon, lettuce and tomato
sandwich and potato chips. (I still get teased for that one.)
Before we were married, we discussed our plans for
having children. I had always dreamed of having two children-
a boy first and a girl second - four years apart. Gary and I
both thought that would be ideal! So that's what I ordered! I
figured if I'm what my parents ordered, maybe it would work
for us. Of course, we were going to wait two years before we
started a family. We both had jobs and wanted to get
established and have some money before we added little ones
to our family. We thought it would be a good idea to get to
know each other better as husband and wife. If I remember
right, it was six months later during a duck dinner I had
prepared (Wow! Far cry from B.L.T.'s) that Gary said, "Let's
have a baby!" Well a month later the idea became a reality. I
was pregnant. I am not going to detail my nine months of
pregnancy. But, the time waiting and the delivery were not

easy. Through many prayers by a wonderful family and Christian friends, a faithful husband, and a precious mother who stayed close by through three days of labor, a week at home, and then back into the hospital, our first child, Darren Ward was born weighing 8 pounds 3 ounces on March 28, 1969. My mother stayed as close as she could in the father's waiting room.   I would like to share parts of a little note she wrote to me when problems were arising in the labor room.

"Dearest Darling Nan",

Honey, there isn't too much I can say right now and I'm as close to you as they will let me be. Don't fret and worry, just keep in mind the Lord has already timed the coming of your little one. Just remember, put your trust in the Lord and completely rest in Him. Remember the most precious gifts, don't always come easy.

I love you,

Mom

God had answered my prayer for I had ordered a son.
I was anxious to get home and start our happy times together with our new little son. The morning of the day we were to be dismissed from the hospital, I went to look through the nursery window at my little bundle of joy in his basket. But he wasn't there! I looked around thinking the nurses had moved his crib. Fortunately, my parents were standing beside me as a tear came from my eye down my cheek. "Where is my baby?" I asked. We then found out from the nurse that Darren had jaundice and would not get to go home with us. He would have to stay in an incubator for four or five days until his problem was better. His little skin was so yellow, and when I looked into his eyes (which were starting to open more) the whites of his eyes were completely yellow. "Oh Lord, please take care of our little Darren. He's just what we ordered and please help his blood count to go down so we can take him home with us and be a happy family of three."
I was nursing my baby, which was a special part of being a mother. Even though we left him at the hospital I

would go back and feed him when I could. Finally after four days, which seemed like forever, Darren came home. His father was so proud to have a son!

I quit my job at the bank because I had also told the Lord unless I absolutely had to work when I had children I did not want to work outside of the home. I wanted to be a full time mommy and spend my days with our son. God blessed Gary with a good job as an electrician so I could do that. Our home of three blessed my heart. And in thankfulness to the Lord for our son Darren, we gave him back to God when he was three weeks old at a dedication service at our church. His grandfather, affectionately called Papa, led in this precious time in our lives, and made us aware it was a time to appreciate God's gift to us.

LESSON 6

YOUR PROBLEMS CAN BE OPPORTUNITIES

BUT HE GIVETH MORE GRACE. WHEREFORE HE SAITH,
GOD RESISTETH THE PROUD, BUT GIVETH GRACE
UNTO THE HUMBLE. JAMES 4:6 (KJV)

As a young mother I tried to spend all the time I could with our little son. He was growing so fast! I wanted to enjoy each day to its fullest. Trips to the beach in the summer to play in the sand, teaching Darren to ride a tricycle, taking him to grandparents' for a visit, and most of all reading him Bible stories and singing songs of Jesus' love as I tucked him into bed each night were special times for us.

Gary and I knew we needed to stay active in the Lord's work. I continued to work with teens in our church. We were Youth Directors. I was the teen Sunday School teacher and also led in our Acteen group for girls and the Women's Missionary Union. I continued playing the piano and singing for the Lord. During this time in my life I was introduced to an organization called Christian Women's Club. It was a fantastic group of women (all denominations), coming together to enjoy one another's Christian fellowship for lunch, music, a special feature program, and a special speaker each month. It was a great opportunity to take my non-Christian friends to hear the gospel in a non-threatening way. I became involved working on the board and then was asked to become chairman of a new group that had just begun. It was a very busy time of my life with a little child, but Darren always went with me. I can remember one of the speakers at a luncheon brought out a point I have always remembered and try to concentrate on in time of changes and problems. "Do not think of your problems as problems - but opportunities."

That really helps my outlook on my everyday detours and changes in life. It gives me more of a positive outlook to cope. I did not know I would be able to put that lesson into practice right away. Gary talked to me one day about having "our girl" at that time. It surprised me, because he knew our children were supposed to be four years apart. That's what I ordered! So we kind of put the idea on hold. I continued my daily life being mother to our one and a half year old son. Darren was healthy and a chubby little guy. For a nickname, his Aunt Net (Janette) called him "Tubs." As I walked around the house and went about my daily activities I started noticing my back was hurting. The pain progressed as time went on, and my left leg began to feel numb. It was also getting harder to walk. I decided to go to the doctor. After trying medication for a month the problem did not go away. I was told I had to have a Myelogram, a test which they inject fluid into the spine. It was a tedious test but needed to be done to find my problem. The doctor made the appointment at a nearby hospital and said I was to have it done as an outpatient. There would be no problems. "The only thing that might occur is a severe headache, that only happens to one out of five people," he said. (Now when Myelograms are performed you are either hospitalized or remain flat on your back for twelve hours.)

I arrived at the hospital, had the test and was told to wait a half hour and I would be O.K. and could go home. A friend of mine, Marie Cleaveland, took me to the hospital so I would not have to drive home. I laid in the back seat of the car to keep my back straight for a while longer. I couldn't wait to get home because it was somewhat of a tense ordeal. We picked Darren up from where he was staying and I was all ready to put him down for his afternoon nap. We had moved two times since living in our little farm house and lived in an apartment with fourteen stairs to the bedrooms and bathroom. So, when I got home, I walked up the stairs to put Darren in his bed. Suddenly I had a pain come across my forehead and then it moved around the back of my head. I had never felt anything like it. I decided to take a couple of aspirins and lie down for awhile while Darren was sleeping. I thought a little rest might be good before I prepared supper for when Gary got home from work. I did fall asleep for awhile, but when it was time to get up, I couldn't raise my head. I felt like I had just been run over by a Mack Truck. "Lord, what do I do now?" I could hear Darren awake and playing in his bed. I knew that wouldn't last very long. He would be hungry and I would need to go to him. How helpless I felt. Each time I raised my head, pain would shoot down the back of my head. My first step was to call a neighbor, who happened to be a dear friend, Sandy Martz, my choir director from high school. Sandy had become a Christian while living in my parent's home the year I was away at college. She encouraged me in the field of music and as a special sister in Christ.

Fortunately I had a phone by the bed, so I called her to see if she could come to my rescue. She came over right away to take care of Darren until Gary came home. Sandy was a single gal and had not had a lot of experience with little babies, but Darren was a year and a half. I thought it would be no problem for a few hours.

My parents lived in Tennessee then. They had moved when Darren was six weeks old. Dad felt the Lord wanted him to minister there. It was a very hard move for all of us. But, this too helped me to depend on God and on my husband more. Gary's parents lived close by, but his mother worked everyday. It was just a few weeks since I had heard the words: "Think of your problems as opportunities." As I lie flat on my back wondering what to do next, I kept asking myself and God, "How can I make this into an opportunity?" Well, I knew it would only be a few hours and I would be up and at it and as good as new! Sandy encouraged me to phone the doctor. When I told him about the pain he said, "Oh, I'm so sorry Nancy, you happened to be that one out of five, I guess. Just stay down flat and whatever you do don't raise your head. Sometimes these headaches last up to ten days." I thought, well, I'm going to beat this one. There is no way I can stay flat. I have a house to keep and most of all a little son to take care of. But, I didn't beat it! I couldn't raise my head. The pain was awful! Even with medication the headaches just needed to wear off.

After ten days, yes, ten days my headaches left. This was one time I didn't enjoy being a statistic! I finally realized the opportunities I had: I had the opportunity to share my son with several people as they took care of him. I had the opportunity to let others prepare meals and clean our apartment. I had the opportunity to be helpless without my mother around to help me. The idea of someone waiting on me - bathing me and tending to my personal needs was very humbling. But the greatest opportunity of all, I had nowhere to look but up! I had no excuses that I didn't have time to talk to the Lord or "look" to Him. So I took advantage of this time in my life to concentrate on the Lord and let Him know how thankful I was for His many blessings to me. I had plenty of time to pray for the needs of family and friends and to practice James 4:6 -"But He giveth more grace. Wherefore He saith, God resisteth the proud, but giveth grace unto the humble." (KJV)

      The ten days had passed. I was never so happy to be able to stand. The headache was gone and I had an appointment to find out the results of the Myelogram. The doctor gave me the news that I had a ruptured disc, probably a result of carrying Darren around on my hip as most mothers do. Being a heavy little guy, he put too much pressure on my back. I appreciated that my doctor really was not one to perform surgery at the drop of a hat. He said he was going to try some other measures first. He put me in a plaster body cast for three months. Oh, it was so attractive! I was able to walk, sit, and go about my daily routine, but he gave me one warning, "Watch what you eat. This cast does not expand!" Wouldn't you know it? It was coming close to Thanksgiving season and I had to watch my waistline. But if it worked, I didn't mind. Darren had to learn to walk more on his own and it was very hard at times for him to understand why mommy wouldn't pick him up. When it was time for the cast to be "sawed off" of me, I experienced a little of how it must feel to be a magician's assistant when they start coming toward you with a saw. Except this saw was electric! Only time would tell if my back had improved. I was told this would not be a good time to get pregnant again. It would be too much pressure on my back to carry a baby, especially if it were another eight pounder. The next step of treatment was to be fitted for a body corset with metal staves and ties just like in the olden days. I needed to continue using the corset for at least two years. Gary's idea of having another baby was put on hold.

LESSON 7

GOD'S TIMING IS THE BEST TIMING

REJOICE EVERMORE. PRAY WITHOUT CEASING. IN
EVERYTHING GIVE THANKS; FOR THIS IS THE WILL OF
GOD IN CHRIST JESUS CONCERNING YOU.
1 THESSALONIANS 5:16-18 (KJV)

Life as a threesome was great!   We made trips to
Tennessee to visit Nannie and Papa. Teaching Darren how to
fish - our favorite pastime - was a new adventure for father
and son. When Darren was six months old my brother and his
wife adopted a son, Jimmy. He came to them at eight days
old. We had so much fun with the two little guys.

Darren was just a little over three years old when it was
time to have another check on my back problem. The doctor's
words were, "Well Nancy, your back has improved some, but I
just have one thing to say - if you plan on having one more
child, now is the time. We will be taking a chance, but I will
put you on a thousand calorie diet for the full nine months. I
only want you to gain ten pounds. I'm sure you won't have
another eight pound baby that way." We were informed one
more child would be all I could have. There was a possibility I
would have to be put in traction after the delivery.

One month later I was pregnant. I did pretty well at
watching my weight, although it was very hard. I knew it was
important to do as the doctor said. During the time of my
pregnancy I kept hoping and praying the Lord would answer
my prayer and give us a little girl. He had already worked out
a plan for our children to be four years apart. (Although I
would not have chosen His way of delaying my pregnancy.)
But, if I had not gone through the back problem, some more
valuable lessons would not have been learned.   For instance,
1 Thessalonians 5:16-18 says, "Rejoice evermore. Pray
without ceasing. In everything give thanks; for this is the will
of God in Christ Jesus concerning you." These verses
became a living truth during my time of need.

During my ninth month pregnancy check up I was
asked to step on the scale as usual. (Remember I was only

supposed to gain ten pounds.) Well, the scale came up to a fourteen pound weight gain. Was my doctor upset with me! Three weeks later he apologized when an eight pound three ounce baby girl was born. I had had problems in the labor room again and was sent home for two more weeks of contractions. My mother came up to stay with us. She took care of Darren and also kept an eagle eye on me since I was determined I would not go back to the hospital until the very last minute! When I realized I had waited almost too long, it was hard for her to convince Gary he'd better hurry and get me to the hospital. He had spent so many hours, even days waiting before, he was in no hurry to "hurry up and wait again". But, when he saw me doubled over with pains every two minutes, he RACED to the hospital in the next town!

After taking me in to be admitted by the waiting nurse, he thought he would leave for a few minutes thinking, "I have plenty of time!" But did I surprise him! I had done what I said I would do - wait until the last minute. He almost missed the whole event! At 3:04, on April 26, 1973, our 8 pound 3 ounce baby daughter was born. The weight signifies "God gives us only what we can bear". The doctor was surprised that the amount of weight was the exact amount as our first child.

Even though we had ordered our little girl, my faith was not as strong as Gary's. I would doubt at times and say, "Oh, I hope this baby is a little girl." Gary would say, "It is a little girl." He was the only one absolutely certain. So, when Dawn Lee was born I was so happy. The nurse and I decided to be a little mischievous. At that time the husbands were not allowed to be with the wife in the delivery while the baby was being born. So, Gary did not know if we had a little boy or girl until the nurse took the baby out to him in the father's waiting area. She said, "Let's play a little trick on your husband. He was so certain you were carrying a little girl. Let's wrap Dawn Lee in a blue blanket." So she carried Dawn outside into the hall. When Gary realized his new baby had arrived, he walked up to the nurse with a face aglow and a big grin and said, "Take that blue blanket off my little girl." We couldn't fool him! The nurse put her in a little soft pink blanket and handed her over to her father. I guess the verse, "Now faith is the substance of things hoped for, and the evidence of things not seen," was a big part of Gary's life.

Dawn Lee had many visitors while she was in the hospital. When her Aunt Net saw her little red chubby face with three chins and gobs of black hair already long enough for a big curl on top, she said, "She looks like a little papoose with a sunny face. I'm going to call her Sunni." To this day she is the only one who can call Dawn Lee, Sunni.

Everyone was waiting for our big day to go home, especially Darren. He was now four years plus one month old. How's that for timing? He was in preschool and already had all kinds of things in mind to teach his little sister. I was not able to nurse our daughter because of the possibility of having to stay in traction for my back after delivery. But I made it through with no major problems. Dawn and I both were ready to go home.

Our family was complete.

Right away I had all kinds of help from big brother. He wanted to hold his little sister, show her picture books, and tell her stories he had learned at school. He even tried to feed her beets, which to this day she will not eat! But, when it came time to rock her and give her a bottle that was my special time alone with Dawn. Darren always knew and understood.

Most every night I would sing:

DAWN LEE IS MY LITTLE BABY
THE APPLE OF MY EYE
SHE'S DADDY'S LITTLE PRINCESS
BIG BROTHER IS ALWAYS BY HER SIDE.
SHE'S PRECIOUS AS AN ANGEL
SHE'S OUR LITTLE GIRL,
BUT MOST OF ALL WE ALL KNOW
SHE'S GOD'S LITTLE PEARL.

Then she would fall asleep in my arms.

LESSON 8

YOU DON'T HAVE TO GO TO AFRICA TO BE A MISSIONARY

THIS IS MY COMMANDMENT, THAT YE LOVE ONE ANOTHER, AS I HAVE LOVED YOU. JOHN 15:12 (KJV)

It was a Wednesday, 1976, 6:45 p.m. It could have been any Wednesday evening because every Wednesday Sharon Cunningham and I took turns driving to Acteens at church. Remember, this was the organization I was in when I felt the call to be a missionary. I had continued working with Acteens since I was eighteen. Sharon was a very special friend who shared a love for teenage girls, and wanted to teach them about missionaries, Christ's love, and just growing up. We both had many opportunities to offer our shoulders to cry on when the girls had problems that they needed to share.

In our Acteen group we planned some exciting projects and ministries. One of the most important and fulfilling times in our Acteen work was to go and visit Betty Reich. She was a very special lady at a nearby nursing home. Betty was born with cerebral palsy. She was forty years old when we met her. Betty could not use her hands very well and often had a hard time walking. She could not speak to us except by communicating with a rug. When she was a young girl she found out through the help of a friend she could talk by pointing with her foot to letters placed on a rug piece. So we decided we would start making rugs for Betty to help her talk. We would write the alphabet in large printed letters and placed a yes, no, and question mark at the bottom of a rug piece. Betty may have looked like she was not bright, but she was a very bright, enthusiastic, loving, Christian lady. And boy could she talk with that rug! Spelling happened to be my forte' in school so we could carry on some pretty good conversations. The girls worked at keeping up with Betty's foot, but you had to be quick because she was quite a talker. She had a wonderful sense of humor. It was such a joy to go visit her and sometimes take her on an outing. At first we thought we were ministering to Betty, but Betty was truly ministering to us.

I would always come away wondering why I ever complained of my aches and pains. Here was a person who never was able to run and play; she could never be independent and do so many things we take for granted. Betty was a person who was determined to overcome a very debilitating disease. She painted plaques and knick knacks with a brush between her toes. She could type with a wooden spoon between her toes. But most of all she could smile like no one else I've ever seen. (Especially when I fed her baked beans, one of her favorite foods.) The Acteens truly learned so much from our dear friend.

As I continued working with teens, I asked myself the question, "When am I going to become a missionary? Lord, when are you going to call Gary and me to be fulltime missionaries?" These questions kept coming to my mind. I would even "worry" that we weren't where God intended us to be. "Why hasn't Gary given his life completely to you, Lord? What will it take to change him ?" I'd ask.

But time continued on. Sharon and I took the girls to National Conferences in Texas, Kansas City, and Tennessee. We would study about, pray for, and give to missionaries. We even saw some of our girls do mission work. But was that enough? I thought back on that log at Happy Hollow Camp years ago when I prayed, "His Way Mine." I thought it meant I would be appointed a fulltime missionary by a mission board. "I've been praying that Gary would change. I've even tried to change him myself Lord!"

It was the year of the Bicentennial - 1976. I decided it would be a great idea to have the teens perform a musical, "The Fabric of Freedom". It was a wonderful portrayal of how our country became a free country through the time of war, rebuilding homes, and the bond of family. So we worked very hard and presented the musical several times. It was a joy to see how God used this presentation. I learned a special lesson from it. In the summer of 1976 after we had presented "The Fabric of Freedom" to several churches, Gary and I took the teens to Ridgecrest Conference Grounds in the mountains of North Carolina to a teen conference. All of our expenses were paid from love offerings taken at our performances. It was a fun time but most of all inspirational.

The last evening, a missionary spoke and gave an invitation for those who felt God calling them to be missionaries to come forward. My heart skipped a beat. I knew this was it. Lord, you planned a special time. Gary and I were not sitting together because he and the guys were on another row. But that was O.K. I had heard missionary couples' testimonies where they told of how God spoke to them at the same time and they weren't sitting by each other. I'll wait for him to make the first move, then I'll go. I kept looking toward the front. No Gary. Soon the service ended. That was our chance. I thought it was a perfect time to say, "We'll be fulltime missionaries." When I looked for Gary afterward he was not in the building. As I walked outside I saw him sitting alone in a beautiful prayer garden. I don't know if he even heard all of the sermon, because he had been there for awhile. But he was having his own time with the Lord. I don't know if God even spoke to Gary and said "I want you to be a fulltime missionary," But the Lord let me know right then, I had been wrong to try to change my husband into what I wanted him to be. If God wanted us to serve together as missionaries He would call us both, not just one.

I then thought of Acteens, the work Sharon and I were doing, and the lives we were touching in missionary training. Wasn't that being missionaries at home? What about my neighbors? Did they all know the Lord? I remember a question I had heard asked by a missionary speaker. "How can you go overseas if you can't even go across your street?"

Thank you, Lord, for reassuring me I'm where you want me to be.

LESSON 9

GOD ANSWER'S SPECIFIC PRAYERS

AND ALL THINGS, WHATEVER YE SHALL ASK IN PRAYER, BELIEVING, YE SHALL RECEIVE. MATTHEW 21:22 (KJV)

We had lived in five different places in ten years. Gary and I decided we needed to buy a place of our own instead of renting, especially since Darren and Dawn were getting older and had to share a bedroom. We started to put away some money for a down payment, but with just one salary coming in we could not afford the high priced homes on the market.

One of my friends and I had been using prayer baskets during our daily devotions. Kathy lived in another town twenty miles away but we both prayed at 8:30 each morning for each other's needs. When we had a request we would write them on a card and place them in our baskets. One day I told her we needed to pray for a three bedroom, $32,000 house in Liberty Township, the area we wanted to live in. Each day for three months we included this request in our prayers, believing God would answer our specific prayer. Gary thought we were a little "silly" putting a price tag on it, but we believed God would do it, in HIS time.

During the three months we watched the newspapers and looked at several houses with our realtor, but all of the prospects were too high, or not in the right location.

One Saturday morning our realtor called and said, "There's an auction going on at one o'clock in Liberty Township. The people are selling antiques and their house. Would we be interested?"

Neither Gary nor I had ever been to an auction, but we said we would be there just to check it out. We arrived a little before the auction started. The children were with us as we spent ten minutes going through the little three bedroom ranch on a half acre lot. After seeing the house we went outside to the back yard. Gary looked at us and said "If this is the house your mom has been praying for everyday, we'll bid on it, but we won't go over $32,000." Right there we held hands and prayed, "Lord, please show us the way." Since we had never even bid on a tea cup at an auction, we were a little apprehensive, or afraid we'd scratch our head or swat at a fly and buy something we really didn't want. All we were interested in was the house!

There were probably over one hundred people standing and sitting around the front yard. It was time for the bidding on the house to begin. "Do I hear $28,000 to open the bid.?" Gary raised his hand. " Do I hear $29,000?" A tall man on the other side of the yard raised his hand. " How about $30,000?" Gary raised his hand. "Do I hear $31,000?" It was just two of us bidding on the house. As we looked across the lawn, we recognized the other person was Mr. Sutton, a Christian man who used to go to the church where we attended. He could not see us since we both are only 5'5" and 5'6", but the auctioneer continued. "How about $32,000?" Oh Lord, this is it! This is the amount we decided on - the amount we claimed for our little dream house. We had the bid. But wait a minute, the auctioneer said "o.k. Do I hear $32,100?" Mr. Sutton raised his hand. The next question came to us as the auctioneer looked our way. "Do I hear $32,200?" Gary looked at me and I at him. With a smile he shook his head NO. My heart skipped a beat. I could have been sad, but we both knew we had done what God wanted us to do. We said we would not bid over $32,000, so we kept our promise as the Lord had done for us many times in our lives.

We went over to congratulate Mr. Sutton. He said, "I didn't know it was you kids bidding against me. I feel bad." We told him not to worry about it and we were happy for him.

And we were not disappointed, because we knew God was in control. Our dream house would become a reality some day.

The next day was Sunday. It was 8:30 a.m. I'll never forget the time. We were getting ready to go to church when the phone rang. It was Mr. Sutton. He said, "I didn't sleep at all last night. I thought about you kids and how it would be great for you to have that little house. The children would be able to go to school just a half mile from the house. It would be so nice to raise them in the country and I just bought the house for an investment. I'll sign the house over to you for

$32,100." We jumped for JOY, (and we didn't think the Lord would quibble over $100.00). Yes, "Jesus is the same yesterday, today and forever." Hebrews 13:18.

Three weeks later, we met with Mr. Sutton at the bank to sign the papers. We shared our story with the banker, and several others since, hoping to let people know that God is a God of miracles - not just in the Bible, but also today.

We called our little $32,(100) house in Liberty Township - THE BEAVER'S BLESSING.

LESSON 10

THE POWER OF PRAYER IS AMAZING

GREATER IS HE THAT IS IN YOU, THAN HE THAT IS IN THE WORLD. 1 JOHN 4:4b (KJV)

Our little house needed a lot of work done to it. We had only looked through it very quickly the day of the auction and did not notice some of the bad points, problems, or needed improvements.   We only knew it was OURS!

After we moved in, we realized there was not a closet in Darren's bedroom. There was a hole in the wall with a plate covering it where the pot belly stove used to be in the living room. There was chipped tile in the kitchen and bathroom floors and the house was not insulated. But the biggest problem was when we went downstairs, we realized there was no hot water heater. There never had been one. WOW! Our work was cut out for us. We decided to look at the major overhaul as a FUN challenge.

After a few weeks, tearing out walls, stripping old woodwork, building closets, and tackling many other projects were no longer fun. It was hard work! It was winter time and nearing the holidays, but that didn't stop us from digging into the inside renovation.

Everyday, with a mask over my face, I began to strip the old paint and varnish off of the woodwork. Ten to twelve hours a day I would sing a muffled song through the mask, trying to keep my spirits up as I thought of the beautiful wood under all of the yellowed paint. The kids helped out as much as they could, when they were not at school or until something better came along, like going to a friend's house or sledding down the hill in back of our house.

We worked diligently everyday trying to get our dream house presentable for the Christmas holidays. We knew we had a long way to go, but every improvement helped. The project was coming along pretty well. About mid October I started having bad headaches, and strange things started happening. My vision became blurry. I dropped things every once in a while, and I was always tired. Even after a good night's rest. I made an appointment to see my doctor. He prescribed some medication thinking it could be sinus problems, which I had had all of my life. I continued working on the house, but I had to slow down a little because of the medication and the other symptoms that were occurring. It was this time in my life that I met my precious friend Patricia Conaway. We had known of each other in earlier years through church work and Christian Women's Club, but we were not close until a serious illness attacked Patricia. She was hospitalized with a severe attack, causing blindness in her left eye and paralysis to part of her body. She was diagnosed as having Multiple Sclerosis. It was through visiting her at the hospital, praying with her and being there for her that we grew to become lifelong friends. It was during one of my hospital visits that I went to the coffee shop to get a coke. While waiting for Patricia to wake up from a nap, the Lord showed me another lesson as I penned this poem on a napkin.

AS I SIT HERE IN A COFFEE SHOP
SIPPING ON A COLA,
I THINK OF ALL THE THINGS I HAVE TO DO.
THE HECTIC DAY AHEAD OF ME WITH PLANS ALL
DOWN ON PAPER,
AND WONDERING IF THE DAY WILL SEE ME THROUGH.

WITH A HEART A FLUTTER AND ANXIOUS FEELINGS
MY MIND RACED ON.
THEN SUDDENLY I LOOKED TO MY LEFT
A WONDER TO BEHOLD.
A BLIND YOUNG MAN ALL DRESSED IN WHITE,
A NURSE SO I WAS TOLD.

HOW COULD I LORD GET SO UPTIGHT
WITH PROBLEMS OF MY OWN-
WHEN THIS YOUNG MAN JUST STRIVES SO HARD
TO FIND A CUP ALONE,
AS HE COUNTED HIS MONEY TO PAY
THE GIRL HE OWED
HE SMILED AND THANKED HER GRACIOUSLY
WITH A PRECIOUS GLOW.

BUT THEN I REALIZED HOW HE COPED
WITH SUCH A HANDICAP,
HE BOWED HIS HEAD AND MOVED HIS LIPS
TO THANK THE LORD ABOVE-
OH THANK YOU JESUS FOR SHOWING ME
TO TAKE TIME - REACH OUT - AND LOVE.

I realized no matter what my problems were, there is always someone with a larger one than mine. The reason I bring up Patricia's illness now is some of my symptoms were the same as hers, but not as serious. I dropped things, and walked with a slow gait. So, I started wondering - could I have M.S. too? I had been sent to several specialists by my family doctor, searching for some answers. A neurologist prescribed Dilantin for me to take, trying to rule out a brain tumor. I had had every type of x-ray and test imaginable. I was so tired of going from doctor to doctor not getting any answers, just medicine to eliminate the symptoms, only to find out later the medications were causing some of the symptoms. My sweet mother kept saying, "I bet it has something to do with you using that strong stripper to remove the paint with not enough ventilation." Oh, everyone thought that couldn't be. I mean, I always wore a mask. Even when I mentioned to the doctors what I had been doing the past few months, it didn't seem to have a bearing on their diagnosis. They didn't have a diagnosis! My mind started to wander. What do I have? What is wrong with me? Could it be all in my head? The medications made me so drowsy, and everyday I was getting worse instead of better.

I finally decided to make an appointment at Mayo Clinic in Minnesota. By the time I arrived there for my appointment my feet were just shuffling along from being so weak. My mother drove me there and stayed with me while Gary stayed home with the children and worked. My appointment was the week of Thanksgiving. My prayer was to find out what was wrong with me and for Mom and I to be home for Thanksgiving dinner with our family. For three days all kinds of tests were taken, some I had even had before. By Wednesday afternoon the final results and consultation was scheduled. I met with the doctor and heard what he had to say. One of the blood tests verified I had some lead poisoning in my system, probably from the combination of the chemicals and old paint I was stripping off of the woodwork the past few months. My mother was right! All of the medications I had been put on by various doctors and worrying about the uncertain had caused my muscles to weaken. The physical therapist said my neck and shoulder muscles were like a seventy year olds. So, I had to learn how to build myself back up, physically and mentally. I learned at that time how important the mind is as a part of my body.

I think back on this incident in my life and realize Satan can use tricks to bring us down. He can cause us not to trust in the Lord. He can rob us of our JOY if we let him. He can cause our minds to wonder and bring us down in so many ways. But with Christ's Spirit in me and because of the prayers of many people, I won the battle. "Greater is He that is in you, than he that is in the world." 1 John 4:4b. Through heat treatments, exercises and going off the strong medication I did not need, (and staying away from furniture stripper) I started on the road to recovery. Oh, by the way, Mom and I left Rochester, Minnesota during the night in a terrible snowstorm with four feet of snow. We arrived at my brother's home on Thanksgiving Day - just as the family was sitting down for the blessing. They were all surprised we had made it, and yet they all somehow knew, as we held hands and prayed, that God had once again answered our prayers.

LESSON 11

LIVING EVERYDAY TO ITS FULLEST
IS MAKING MEMORIES

ENTER INTO HIS GATES WITH THANKSGIVING, AND INTO
HIS COURTS WITH PRAISE; BE THANKFUL UNTO HIM,
AND BLESS HIS NAME. FOR THE LORD IS GOOD; HIS
MERCY IS EVERLASTING, AND HIS TRUTH ENDURETH
TO ALL GENERATIONS. PSALMS 100: 4-5 (KJV)

Christmas was a very special time at our house. Each
year Darren and Dawn would get so excited about picking out
a Christmas tree, decorating, and finding an unusual outfit to
wear on Christmas Eve. Some years they would wear their
new Christmas pajamas with Santa Claus hats from when
they were little babies. Some outfits included long striped
socks and silly slippers. But no matter what they came up
with, they had fun as dad took their picture together in front of
our beautiful fireplace, designed and built by my brother, Jim.
Every Christmas Eve the Beaver's family celebrated at our
house. My family, (Mills) took turns at each other's house on
Christmas morning. This time with my parents, my brother,
sister-in-law, and two nephews, Jimmy and Jason, was very
special. Jason was our "little miracle" baby - born to Jim and
Janette eight years after Jimmy arrived. Being so much
younger than the other children, he really got the attention!
Jim and Janette also took care of their two foster
daughters, sisters Kathy and Char. They were very special to
all of us during their four years with Jim and Janette. We had
great family fellowship opening presents, eating, singing
around the piano CELEBRATING CHRIST'S BIRTHDAY. It
has always worked out real well to be able to share our time
without conflicts.
Gary has two younger brothers, Dennis and Craig.
Dennis and his wife Karen married in their early twenties.
About two years after they were married they decided to be
house parents for the Baptist Children's Home. Their
assignment was a family of seven, one boy and six girls, all
from one family. The children were put in the home because

their mother died of cancer and their father was an alcoholic. The mother's wish before she died was for the children to stay together. Dennis and Karen also had a baby of their own, my nephew Corey. So they took on the big challenge of being newlyweds and raising eight children ages three through sixteen. They felt this was something God wanted them to do.

Karen was an only child and had only a few months to practice cooking for two. I have always given her a lot of credit for learning to cook and clean for that many people. The children were all a big help. They had their daily chores and schedule to keep. A few years later, their second son, Kurtis was born - making a family of eleven!

Gary's youngest brother, Craig, his wife Marian and their three children Jason, Jamie, and Jeremy lived in Oklahoma. We were not able to be with them during the holidays, but a phone call was always in order.

Christmas Eve was so exciting! With all of the foster nieces and nephews and our own children, our house jumped with excitement! The traditional h'or doeuvres at Uncle Gary and Aunt Nancy's changed from year to year, but we always had to have shrimp cocktail. That was a standing request. The most important part of our Christmas time together, both Christmas Eve and Christmas Morning was the reading of the Christmas story from the second chapter of Luke in the Bible. All of the hustle and bustle from holiday preparation ceased as we listened quietly with thankful hearts about Christ's wonderful birth. Every year tears filled both Grandpa Beaver's and Papa Mills' eyes as it was their privilege to share this reading with us. After our company would leave every Christmas Eve, Gary would read "Twas the Night Before Christmas" as the milk and cookies were left on the mantle for a special visitor.

Birthdays were also special memories . Each year when it was Darren's and Dawn's birthdays, they would choose the kind of cake they wanted to have for their party. Even though I was not a professional cake decorator, I enjoyed trying my hand at things such as The Lone Ranger, cowboys and Indians, wrestlers, PacMan, clowns, gymnastics, baseball and Barbie to name a few. Some of the creations were even questioned. "Uh Mom, what is this supposed to be?" With a smile I would say, "Remember, it's what's inside that counts!" Most of the time it was chocolate!

Every summer was filled with little league. Gary coached Darren's teams for eight years. It was a very busy time, but most of all, it was fun and a time to build a lasting father and son relationship. Dawn played softball also, so we spent many hours on bleachers and in the concession stand selling candy. Vacation Bible School would end the summer break. Then school would start, and we would spend more hours on bleachers during school sports. I would not trade those memories in for anything. Little did I know how fast the years would go by.

I would always make time for special friends. While sharing cups of tea with my dear friend, Brenda Beal, she taught me to be a little "bolder" and helped me to have more self confidence. I was so busy in church work and with family. My special friends Patricia Conaway, Sharon Tarry, and my sister-in-law, Janette, decided we should have a time together once a month to just enjoy one another's company. It was not a time for meetings or planned business, but a time to relax and unwind - which all young mothers need to do. We cooked special recipes and made little gifts to show our friendship. We called it JOYTIME. We knew the meaning of JOY - Jesus first, Others second, and Yourself last. What a blessing to have dear friends!

Our family would also try to fit in trips to Kentucky and Tennessee to visit relatives. Those times were very special for me. I wanted to show the kids how important it was to keep in touch and renew fellowship with family and friends, even though miles separated us. As we went back to Kuttawa, Kentucky, my mother's birthplace, we would visit my aunts, uncles and cousins. It was not the same as I remembered as a child, but I would share my childhood memories with Darren and Dawn. We had good times at Aunt Norm's house on the mountain. I have memories of drawing water from the well, sleeping with my cousins on a feather bed thrown on the floor, and getting coal for the stove. My fondest memory was playing church on the front porch. It was always a BIG decision between myself and my three cousins, Anita,

Linda, and Gary Paul, as to who would be the preacher, song leader, and pass the offering plate!

It was so hard for Darren and Dawn to believe that's the way it was, because times had changed. But they could get a taste of the Old Kuttawa and my childhood as we walked along the new street above the flooded town. The Tennessee Valley Authority (TVA) had flooded the old town which is now Barkley Lake. It was kind of sad to see the old drugstore we could get a nickel cone at - gone. But that's the way life is. It never stays the same. It's always changing everyday. As we would pack up our things to go back "up north", I would realize one thing - GOD NEVER CHANGES! We can't stop time, progress, or the changes in the world. But, the Lord can help us to make precious memories as the clock ticks on!

LESSON 12

GOD'S WORD HELPS CALM YOUR SPIRIT

FOR GOD HATH NOT GIVEN US THE SPIRIT OF FEAR,
BUT OF POWER, AND OF LOVE, AND OF A SOUND MIND.
2 TIMOTHY 1:7 (KJV)

      It was a beautiful summer day, kind of hot. I was doing the usual straighten the house, and do the wash type of things. It was great to have Darren and Dawn home for the summer, even though by September 1st, I would probably be ready for them to go back to school. After the little league season was over and playing a couple of weeks out in the country with very few neighborhood children close by, boredom usually set in. But this summer day in 1983, Darren was out riding bikes with a buddy and an exciting challenge came to Dawn. She was ten years old and always loved to play rough and tough. I guess she was a "tomboy of sorts". She had to keep up with the guys since she was the only girl in the family and among our friends. Our next door neighbor boy, David, asked Dawn if she would like to ride his mini bike. There are several acres behind our house with a few sloping hills. But she felt she could handle it since she had mastered a two wheeled bicycle. I was a little nervous because I do not like any type of motorcycles, but David was close by and said it didn't go very fast. I continued my housework until about thirty minutes had passed. As I went outside to hang some clothes on the clothesline, I noticed Dawn was walking toward the house. She wasn't crying but I didn't see the mini bike anywhere and as she neared the back yard it was evident her hand was wrapped around the left side of her neck. I hurriedly met her in the yard and asked her if anything was wrong. She told me what had happened. The mini bike went a little faster than she expected and she lost control, went down a hill and ran into a barbed wire fence. As she took her hand from her neck I could not believe how calm she was. For there was about an inch and a half gap in her neck where some barbed wire had cut her. It was bleeding quite a bit, so I ran into the house to get a cold cloth for her to hold on the wound. When I came back outside I noticed her shirt was torn right in front below her neckline and there was blood around the tear. I pulled the torn piece of material to the side to see if there was another cut on the neck. There was a four inch gap in Dawn's chest. I panicked. I actually fell apart and acted like a crazy woman. Dawn didn't even realize she was cut there. She knew she also had a burn on her leg from it touching something hot on the bike. I started crying and was starting to hyperventilate. Dawn said, "Settle down, Mom, I'm o.k. You're going to have a heart attack." I had always been pretty cool about the sight of blood or taking care of other children's hurts. But when it was my own child I found out how easy it is to fall apart! We went into the house to call the doctor's office to let them know about the accident and that I would bring Dawn in right away, because I was very sure she would need some stitches. We live about six miles from town so I quickly got some more damp towels and helped Dawn hold the cold compresses on her cuts. I wondered if I was able to drive as nervous as I had become. David went home to tell his mom what had happened to Dawn. She felt so bad since it was their bike Dawn was using, but accidents do happen.

I then came to my senses enough to realize I had NO car. Our car was in the shop and Gary had the truck at work. Well, I'll go next door I thought, and ask Jackie, David's mother, if she could drive us to the doctor. She had no car. Our neighbor, Vern, on the corner was home, so I asked him if he could drive us to the doctor's office. I was concerned that maybe I really needed to call an ambulance, but Vern, being a volunteer fireman and knowing first aid treatment, said he thought if we left right away it would be okay. We started for his car and he realized he had a flat tire. I was trying to stay calm, which was very hard after having nearly experienced being in shock. Dawn's control and patience continued to amaze me. Vern then went across the street to another neighbor's house to see if he could borrow their vehicle. We finally got a car and drove to the doctor's office. In the mean time Darren and his friend came home to find us in a rush and we had very little time to give him information about Dawn's mishap. As we drove away the expression on his face was one of worry about his little sister. I yelled out the window,

"She'll be alright. We're on our way to the Dr." We arrived at the emergency entrance and took Dawn into the room they had prepared for her. She calmly sat and waited a few moments more for the doctor to arrive. I tried to carry on a conversation to keep her mind off of the two large cuts she had, but also to keep myself halfway sane. And when I looked up, there stood Darren and his friend. They had ridden their bikes into town to check on Dawn. Minutes seemed like an eternity. When the doctor came in and looked at the places she had been cut he said, "Well, stitches are in order here." As she was draped for what almost looked like major surgery I lasted as long as I could. I was going to try to watch the whole procedure, but decided the attending nurse did not need to get smelling salts out to revive a mother who had fainted. So I waited in the hallway. As I was waiting for them to "sew" Dawn's wounds up, the verse, "For God hath not given us the spirit of fear, but of power, and of love, and of a sound mind." 2 Timothy 1:7 came to mind. I needed to rely on God's Spirit. When the doctor was done, he called me back into the room and said, "we had to put five stitches in Dawn's neck and ten in her chest. I tried to do a good job so all she'll hopefully need is a little Cover Girl to cover the scars when she goes to her Senior Prom." Dawn was still in good shape. She was smiling. Before we left, the doctor came back into the room and told us the cut in Dawn's neck just missed her juggler vein by an inch, and the one in her chest was two inches from the heart. "It's good it wasn't deeper - she's a lucky little girl!" But I knew it wasn't luck at all! The Lord had spared her life and I'm sure for a special reason! Dawn Lee was very strong until the nurse came in with the long needle to give her a tetanus shot. Then the tears began to roll. (I was beginning to think we had a Superwoman on our hands.)

LESSON 13

GOD HOLDS THE KEY TO OUR FUTURE

MY GOD SHALL SUPPLY ALL YOUR NEEDS ACCORDING
TO HIS RICHES IN GLORY. PHILIPPIANS 4:19 (KJV)

As I think back to the beginning of the year 1983, I remember clearing away the holiday trimmings and getting my mind set on a new year. Darren was now finishing the eighth grade and Dawn the fourth. Gary's job as a union electrician working at the steel mills had slowed down gradually. As most construction jobs go, you never can depend on what will come up next, or if anything will come up at all. He was cut back to a couple of days a week and then was notified there was NO work in the area at all. This problem had occurred before and we knew it wouldn't be long. Another job would come up soon. We kept waiting for calls from his boss to tell us it was time to go back to work. Three months passed, six months passed. I was still a homemaker and we had decided that was the way we wanted it to stay, since I felt it was important to be there for the children. We were starting to get behind in our bills because of very little money coming in. Gary did some odd jobs trying to get some money for us to live on, but everything was slow everywhere.   I was still working with teenagers at church which seemed to be a lifetime calling, but it was hard to keep all of our activities going and do a lot of "extras" because of the lack of money. We kept praying for the phone to ring, telling us this dry spell would end, but it didn't happen.

After six months had passed Gary's unemployment checks had stopped coming. We knew the Lord had a purpose in all of this. For one thing we found out how proud we could be, and then how fast we could become humble. I can remember coming home from church one day and as we opened the door we noticed four bags of groceries sitting on our cabinet. We figured it was probably brought over by my brother or our friends, Sharon and Jim Cunningham. There was no note or trace of who the "angels" were that visited our house.

40

At first Gary was somewhat upset and almost too proud to accept this gift freely. But he knew the food was much needed, especially for two growing children. We found out that one of my Acteens, who had grown up, gone to college and had been newly married, had brought us our "love packages." Denisa Kay Nickell, with her husband, shared their small income by buying the groceries for us. When I approached Denisa to thank her, she hugged me with both of our eyes filled with tears, and said , "This is just appreciation for sharing your lives with me when I was a teen and helping me through decisions and hard times." "My God shall supply all your needs according to His riches in glory." Philippians 4:19.

He supplies our needs in ways we don't even expect. People at church would shake our hands and there would be a ten or twenty dollar bill in our hands afterwards. We praised God everyday for our Christian family and friends.

September came and there was still no work in sight. Nine months had passed. Gary and I had to do some serious talking and possibly make life changing decisions. He had always enjoyed his work of being an electrician. He could try another profession, but after four years of schooling, and fifteen years of his life invested in the trade, we didn't want him to lose his seniority with his company when work picked up and he was called back. The only solution we could see was for me to go to work, but I hadn't worked outside of the home in fourteen years! Then my next thought was, "Well, the children are a little older and becoming more independent, so maybe it would be o.k." I had worked at a bank as a teller for four years before Darren was born. I started mulling through my mind. I had one year of college and had planned to go into elementary education as a teacher. But how could that help me now? I really didn't know where to begin, but something had to be done quickly.

I remembered the year before. I had gone to the administration building for our school system and filled out some applications for job positions. I really didn't know why. At the time I wasn't planning on working outside of the home. But God's plan was starting to unfold. When one of my friends heard I was considering getting a job, she phoned to tell me there was a secretarial job opening at Liberty Middle School where Darren had attended. I stopped by the Vice Principal's office and talked to him about the job opening and my need to work. It was not a formal appointment, but Mr. Eggers did not encourage me to try for the position at their school. He said it would be too hard to cope with Jr. High kids plus learn a job that I had no experience in. He was very nice but honest and had a good point. The adolescent sixth through eighth graders would be a BIG challenge. I was used to working with teens, but in a different setting! He told me I needed to go and update my application on file from the previous year. I went from there to the Administration building to do just that. The next day Mr. Eggers called me and said there was an opening at Jackson Elementary School for an assistant secretary. Jackson was a "country school" about eight miles from our home. I then proceeded to call and make an appointment with Mr. Ken Miller, the principal. An interview time was set up and I was on my way. Oh, was I nervous! I borrowed an outfit from a girlfriend for the interview that looked what I thought would be professional looking. Of course, how would I know what would be appropriate after wearing blue jeans, sweats, and bobby socks, and tennies for the past fourteen years?

I arrived at the two story old historical looking school ten minutes before my appointed time. Mrs. Dolores Kaletha, the head secretary showed me to a bench to wait until I was called. I felt like a little kid who had done something wrong and was waiting outside of the principal's office for my third degree questioning. I must have looked that way too, because as I sat impatiently wringing my hands, the assistant secretary whose position was to be filled came out in the hall and said. "Relax, Honey, you're not at the dentist office!" Just five minutes later, which seemed like an hour, I was told to go into Mr. Miller's office. I had never met Ken Miller before, so that made me even more nervous. He asked me to sit down and proceeded to look over my application. I had heard seventy women had their applications on file for the two secretarial positions. Some were experienced secretaries from steel mills, past legal secretaries, and bookkeepers. I figured I really didn't have much of a chance at the job, but

Gary and I had been praying at home that the Lord would open a door somewhere.

The interview continued with questions regarding my qualifications and background. How many words can you type, have you ever handled money? (I liked that one!) My experience as an office aide all through high school was down on paper. Mr. Miller noticed my experience with children in Sunday School, Vacation Bible School and other church activities. This conversation led to my sharing about being a "preacher's kid". I was still very nervous, but at that point Ken Miller said , "Well I'm a P.K. too." We started sharing a few feelings about what we had in common - our faith in Jesus Christ! It was like a quiet peace went over me. I then went in another room and typed a short letter for Mr. Miller and was told he had several other interviews and he would call me when a decision was made. I really didn't expect to hear right away, but left the final outcome with the Lord. A few days passed, and I had no word about the job. But I hadn't given up hope yet. I just had a feeling! Gary and I both kept praying throughout the week. If Jackson was where God wanted me to help out with the family's income in this time of need , He would provide. A week passed and on a Monday at 5:05 in the evening, the phone rang. It was Mr. Miller. My heart started doing flip flops. Was it a yes or a no? I put my hand over the mouthpiece and said to Gary who was sitting on the couch in front of me, "It's Mr. Miller!" Gary came over to where I was standing. I then heard the words, "Nancy I have decided, you've got the job if you would like it!" You can start next week for a couple of days of training with Ruth, the secretary whose position you are taking." I said "Oh, thank you, I'll see you then." As I hung up the phone, tears of joy flooded my eyes as Gary and I hugged each other while jumping around the kitchen.

I had about four days to get a wardrobe ready - (from what I had in my closet). I was anxious to start, but also very apprehensive as to whether I could handle the job. I really didn't know what all to expect. My main concern was how do I talk to all of those teachers? They are highly educated and have been in the work force for years. I had very little contact with adults, even at church or socially. My time was always given to youth. I was only used to talking to little kids or teenagers. I knew I couldn't walk in the lounge with a greeting of "Hey dude, what's happenin?" I also didn't know all of the responsibilities the job would hold, but my first day of work arrived and I was out the door and on my way.

When I walked through the door of Jackson Elementary School that first morning of work, I knew my life would never be the same. I knew being around the children would be exciting and somewhat similar to my work at church. But, would I be accepted among my peers? It only took five minutes to realize the warmth of the staff at Jackson. I don't know if they were all warned we have a real "greenie" coming aboard or if it just showed, but everyone was there to help me get adjusted and guide me in anyway I needed.

Probably the neatest remembrance of that first day at work was when Ruth Morris, the lady whose position I was filling met with me in my new little office (a converted shower room) and said - Ken and I were praying the Lord would send the right person for this position. And Gary and I were praying at home. She asked if I would like to start the morning off praying together before she showed me the ropes. How exciting! I couldn't believe it. Even though prayer was not allowed in the classroom, I was going to work at a place (a public school) that people were not afraid to pray before they started their work day. Those two days of learning my responsibilities were packed with information and yet, I would learn a lot just by everyday occurrences. I learned real quickly that working at an elementary school would not be boring. Each day was different. You never knew what to expect.

My third day on the job Mr. Miller called me into his office. After asking me to sit down he said, "Nancy, I really don't know why I hired you." I thought, well, that's strange. But he continued. "There were a lot of qualified people who had applied and interviewed for your job, but when I looked back over the applications before deciding who to hire and I came to yours, it felt like electricity went through my body." He didn't try to explain his comment and I didn't try to understand it. I think we both just knew God had answered both of our prayers in an unusual way.

LESSON 14

WITH GOD - THERE'S ALWAYS PEACE DURING THE STORM

GOD IS OUR REFUGE AND STRENGTH, A VERY PRESENT HELP IN TROUBLE.
PSALMS 46:1 (KJV)

I had been working at Jackson Elementary School for a year and enjoyed it a lot. It was hard to adjust my schedule and energy to do all of the housewife and mother duties at home after a day at work, but I tried very hard. My parents were living in Kentucky at that time because Dad was pastor of a church in Princeton, Kentucky. One evening after work I received a phone call from Mom. She didn't seem real upset, but I knew there was something wrong by the way the conversation started. "Nan, I got some news today from the doctor. I had been short of breath a lot and a doctor wanted to check out the cause. After going through several tests they found a hole in my heart that has been there since birth." Right at her appointment time the doctor made arrangements for surgery to be done within a couple of weeks. Mom was sixty-six years old and the doctor was amazed at how long she had lived with this problem. My brother Jim and I decided to go to Nashville, Tennessee, when the surgery took place. The night before our trip I spent several hours thinking about my precious mother and what she meant to me. I wanted to express my love and thoughts about her. So I sat down with my pen and paper and wrote this poem.

MY MOTHER'S MIRACLE

I have always known my Mother is a very special lady,
Her love and care has been shown throughout the years to
everyone-
But especially now the importance of her life is evident,
as we see what God has done.

As a child she suffered many losses, her mother at age seven,
and an only brother too,
but her closeness to God, even then,
seemed to bring her through.

Her dedication to the Lord led Dad to come to Christ,
side by side they've ministered for many years,
for this - there is no price.

As a mother she raised two children
sharing God's word with us each day.
I've seen many tears of joy and concern,
as she would bow to pray.

Her grandchildren call her blessed,
she's such a joy to them.
Her wisdom shared with young ones
has been such a precious gem.

Now we marvel at the news of what the doctor's have to say,
a hole in the center of mom's heart
since birth (sixty-six years ago)
Praise God, she's here today!

The doctor's shake their heads as they are so much amazed,
how mom survived these many years
some say - She's to be praised!

But mom will tell you, it's not me,
it's my Savior from above.
He's watched over me, been In my heart,
and kept me in His love.

With Love, Nancy Lee

I typed, framed and took a copy of the poem to Mom
before her surgery with a bouquet of pink carnations. I wanted
it to cheer her up and help her not to be afraid. But, as usual,
Mom was ministering to us - as her sister Norma was crying
by her side, Mom told us not to be afraid, she had a peace of
mind and heart that God would take care of her and if anything
did happen during surgery, she was ready to be with Jesus.
The surgery went well and many people were touched
by Mom's testimony in the hospital and to those all around.
Many were praying for her. God had many more years of
service and plans for my dear mother and I praise Him for
that. The peace that calmed her storm was an example for
me to always rely on GOD as I faced several storms ahead in
my life.

LESSON 15

GOD HAS A SENSE OF HUMOR -
SO LEARN TO LAUGH AT YOURSELF

A MERRY HEART DOETH GOOD LIKE A MEDICINE.
PROVERBS 17:22a (KJV)

I've done so many "DUMB" things through the years that people have chuckled about. But, boy, were they embarrassing! Fortunately, in time I could laugh at myself. I think back to an incident when Darren was seven years old. One day Gary told me to put a quart of oil in our car, a 1968 Thunderbird. Well, Darren and I had a shopping day planned at a nearby mall. Before our trip I remembered to put the oil in the car. But where? I asked our son, thinking boy's knew about those things. He said as we opened the hood - there's a hole in here somewhere, where Dad puts the oil. So, I found the nearest hole and filled it full. We started the engine and took off for a great day at the mall. After spending several hours window shopping and eating out, we returned to our car. I started the engine, or shall I say tried to start the engine, but it was dead. Well, I thought what could be the problem? The car is full of gas - it should go!

Darren and I decided to walk over to a nearby filling station to have them jump the car so we could get on our way. As we started for home, I noticed smoke coming out of the front of the car. I wondered what could be the problem. We just made it into the driveway. Gary came home from work and as we were eating dinner I told him about the car smoking and not starting. He just happened to ask, "Did you put oil in the car today?" I said "Oh sure." He then said, "Where did you put it?" Now, I don't know why he even asked that question. My reply was, "Darren and I put it in the hole right by that silver thing." He said, "Come show me." As he lifted the hood I pointed to the area where the oil was put. "THE RADIATOR!!! You put oil in the RADIATOR!" Well, that one has been a hard one to live down. (Especially since my father was a past mechanic).

When I started my job at the school there was a list of humorous incidents that followed. Our main office at Jackson was a tiny little area with a desk and several filing cabinets crammed into a small space. Part of my job description was to take care of sick children, or at least check their temperatures when they felt sick. About the third day of work, a little girl came in with a tummy ache. So, I got the thermometer ready to put Into her mouth. After waiting the correct time and reading her temperature I started to put the thermometer into what I thought was a sterilizer. Just as it reached the hole in the appliance Delores, the other secretary yelled, " NO! That's an electric pencil sharpener!" When word got out about that, the whole staff ribbed me for weeks.

One of my requirements at work was to attend a computer workshop at a nearby instructional center. It was in the middle of winter and very cold in Indiana. I was running late the morning of the session. I flew into the meeting, took my coat off, and sat at the computer all ready to learn. The room was filled with a few secretaries and a lot of administrators. About one and a half hours later, a custodian from the nearby high school walked into the room and said, "There is a gray car parked outside with the doors locked and the motor is running." My computer partner and assistant principal at Jackson, Frank Vernallis asked me, "Nancy , is that your car?" I said "No, I wouldn't do that," and smiled. A couple of minutes later, after no one else moved from their chairs Frank said, "Do you have your keys?" I said, "Of course." But, I looked in my purse to be sure and guess what, my keys were not in there. I quickly threw my coat on and ran outside to check to see if it was my car. Sure enough - it was! Oh, another embarrassing situation! I didn't want to go back into the room and face my friends after such another dumb mistake. The only thing I could do was to call home and ask Darren if he had a set of keys to my car. I couldn't reach Gary where he was working, and truthfully I didn't want to! So, I phoned and woke our son up and asked him to come and unlock the door so I could turn the car off. Fortunately it was winter time. It was like an oven in the car when I opened the door. The steering wheel was hot to touch. Heat had been going full blast all that time. I just bowed my head and thanked the Lord that the car didn't blow up! When I returned to my seat at the computer, the leader of the group had told everyone in the room they could only tell two people what had happened. Later I found out the principals told only two people, eye to eye, but there were at least ten or fifteen people standing around them at the time. That afternoon when I returned to Jackson, my desk was piled high with all kinds of keys to commemorate my unforgettable day. What a bunch of jokesters!

I didn't tell Gary about that little episode, but thanks to Dr. Dan Keilman saying two months later when we went to his house for dinner, "Hey Gary, what did you think that day Nancy had the car mishap?" I was shaking my head NO behind Gary's back as I looked at Dr. Keilman. Oh well, I guess it didn't pay to keep a secret. It was good to have someone around who could cheer everyone up with laughter and give them something to laugh at. But sometimes my escapades really were wacky!

LESSON 16

GOD'S LOVE CAN SEE YOU THROUGH ANYTHING

I CAN DO ALL THINGS THROUGH CHRIST WHO STRENGTHENETH ME. PHILIPPIANS 4:13 (KJV)

The year 1987 proved to be a year of trusting in many ways. I was learning to trust as a parent and also to trust as a child of God.

Darren was a senior in high school and Dawn Lee was an eighth grader. Time sure was passing by quickly! Darren had asked us if he could go with three of his buddies to Texas on his spring break. They were going to visit one of his friend's grandparent's house. We really weren't too excited about the idea, but knew we had to start letting go and let him use his "wings". He had just turned eighteen on March 28th, and the boys were planning on leaving the next week. We talked it over and decided to let him go. The van was loaded with suitcases, fishing poles, radios, golf clubs, and even a small T.V. for the get away trip to Texas. I really was starting to hope this wasn't a bad idea - letting them go so far away. But plans had been made and last minute arrangements were all complete. As the guys drove away I said, " I love you Darren - please be careful!" I then said, "Lord, protect them as only you can." Gary didn't seem to worry. Dad's are like that! "You know he's a big boy, Mom. They've got to leave the nest sooner or later," he said with a grin on his face.

We went about our Saturday evening plans and went to bed for a good night's rest. At 3:00 in the morning, I was awakened by a sudden feeling and cold sweats that something was wrong. I couldn't say what, but I knew (as mothers do sometimes) something was wrong with Darren. I sat up in bed and told Gary, but he encouraged me not to worry and to go back to sleep. I could only keep praying, "Lord Jesus, please take care of Darren. Keep him safe." At 7:30 in the morning the phone rang and on the other end was Darren's voice. "Hi mom, I'm calling from a hospital in Arkansas. I'm o.k. though." The boys were taking turns driving and their plan was to drive straight through without stopping overnight. The one boy who was driving in the night fell asleep at the wheel and went off of the road. The van rolled four times. Darren and Dwayne, were taken to the hospital with scrapes and bruises. The other two were unhurt and were taken to a motel by the police. The van was totaled, but four lives were saved. Gary and the father who owned the van drove to Arkansas to bring the boys and all of their belongings home. God watches over us, and He also speaks to us in mysterious ways.

One morning about six weeks after the van accident, I had just settled down at school for a day's work and the phone rang. It was not a parent asking why the school bus was late nor another secretary wanting the lunch count, but it was a long distance call for me from St. Joseph, Michigan. Gary had left two hours before I went to work to travel to Michigan where he had to work. As I answered the phone, I heard Gary's faint voice, "Nan, I've been burned. I'm at a hospital in St. Joe, Michigan. I'm O.K., but get here as soon as you can." My heart was pounding so fast. What should I do next? I had to think fast! I hung up the phone and told my boss I had to leave. Gary was hurt; I didn't know how badly. I called my sister-in-law Janette and told her about it. She said, "I will go with you and drive." Neither one of us had ever been to St. Joe. We had to find out how to get there. I went home, called the schools where the children attended and explained the situation (as much as I knew). I just left town hoping Darren and Dawn could handle everything on the home front, because my wonderful husband needed me by his side. Before I left, Ken Miller my boss walked me to my car and said, "Let's have prayer". Praise God for wonderful Christian family and friends!

It took over an hour to get to St. Joe and find the hospital. It seemed like an eternity! I didn't know how badly Gary was hurt. When I arrived I quickly ran into the hospital to find Gary and the hospital staff waiting for me to come and sign papers for him to be released and transported by ambulance to a Burn Clinic in Kalamazoo, Michigan - fifty miles away. I thought, "Oh no, it must really be bad!" I then found out how the accident happened. Gary was going to burn something with an acetylene torch and it blew up in his hands. He singed his eyebrows and mustache and had second and third degree burns on his chest and around his side and back. When he realized he was on fire from his shirts melting to his chest, he tried to get away from the fire and fell off of a four foot railroad platform and broke his leg. The main concern at that moment in the hospital was if he had inhaled a lot of the fumes and had damaged his lungs. They prepared him to get into the ambulance and Janette followed with our car. I rode in the front with the ambulance driver and must have looked very frightened. He said, "Are you o.k.? Have you ever ridden in a vehicle going ninety miles an hour?" I replied, "No, but whatever it takes, just get us there so they can help my husband."

Gary spent ten days in the burn clinic in Kalamazoo. The first five days were pretty foggy to him because of all of the morphine he needed to be on for pain. It was so hard to see the man I love be so helpless. He was always our strength - the one to make the decisions, the shoulder to cry on. "Please Lord, heal him - spare his life, for me." I not only had to be strong for him, but also for myself. I was in a strange city by myself. I took Janette home after Gary was settled in the hospital, got clothes for myself, checked on our children, and returned that evening to a place I was not familiar with. I had to find somewhere to stay nights. Fortunately, there was a Hospitality House in town where I could stay. Hospital Security Guards saw that I got there safely each evening. I was scared, but knew my favorite verse would once again become real in my life: "I can do all things through Christ who strengtheneth me." Philippians 4:13. Everyday I sat with Gary. They had his leg in a cast and bandages all around his chest and back. He was pretty much sedated, but would come to and hold my hand as we depended on each others' strength to get us through. Each day there seemed improvement. When he went for baths, they took the dressing off and scrubbed all of the old skin off and redressed his burns. At the burn clinic the doctors said it was a blessing that the people at the first hospital didn't try to clean any of the skin off. He probably would have gotten infection and scarred very badly. I was so thankful we were in a place where they seemed to know what they were doing.

The doctors and nurses were so nice and helpful. I would go for walks downtown or down the halls when Gary would sleep. Once in a while thoughts would come in my mind. What if he doesn't live? What would I do? What if he's scarred real bad? What about infection? I asked questions and doubts came into my mind. But, Jesus gave me a peace that Gary was going to be o.k. Gary was in God's hands!

My roommate at the hospitality house was a lady that had many needs. She seemed cold at first. She was there because her grandson was in the hospital. Her whole situation was a very sad case. Her grandson had been into trouble with the law, but while in jail, the sheriff had beaten him with a club until he became brain damaged. He had the mind of a small child, and he was in his early twenties. The grandmother was so bitter. I had an opportunity to talk to her late at night when we returned to our room. The first two nights we didn't speak much - but each night I would read my Bible before I went to sleep. Then I would have a devotion time in the mornings before I would leave for the hospital. I realized God put us together for a reason. Maybe I didn't have the advice and felt like I didn't know what to say to her, but we two became friends. I listened as she shared her bitterness. She respected the time I had with God. She began to ask questions. Why was I so at "peace?" Recil knew there was something different. Why could I handle the situation Gary and I were going through? It was because of Jesus.

Gary began to get stronger and had less pain as the days went by. So many people were praying for him back home. I'll always remember a couple, Bob and Anita (their father was one of our past pastors). They lived in Michigan in a nearby town and they found out we were up there and stopped by the hospital to see me. They couldn't get in to see Gary, but I was so excited to see a face I knew. God had sent them to help relieve my loneliness. He was so good! A day or so after that, Dennis and Karen drove to Michigan to see us. Praise the Lord for a wonderful family! Gary and I also had the opportunity to pray for a little girl who had been burned by spilled hot coffee. She had bandages from head to toe.

She was about two years old. But what was even sadder - her parents never came to see her. She sat in a playpen, or toddled down the hall pulling a little wagon and craved the nurses' attention and love. I realized there were so many cases such as the little burned girl who was not taken care of and the grandson who was abused and hurting. Those patients experienced the pangs of loneliness in a "BIG" world. God puts us in places sometimes to open our eyes to needs around us.

We were given some good news. Gary would not have to have skin grafting done and his skin was healing real well. On the ninth day, the nurse said Gary could go home, but would have to return to the clinic every other day to have his bandages changed. (Which would be a four hour trip every other day.) Or, his alternative decision was I could learn how to bathe him, scrub the skin, and put the dressing on myself and we wouldn't have to make the trip. Well, my experience of nursing at school helped some. I decided I could handle taking care of him at home. That first time I went to see what needed to be done, I was a little queasy, but we managed. I went home from work for one and a half hours every other day and became Gary's nurse. We are so thankful for the "Miracle" of God's healing power and competent medical people who got us through that trying time.

So, 1987 proved to be a very full, interesting year. We survived the two traumatic accidents, the graduation of Darren from high school, and there was a BIG surprise for me at Christmas! One day, just before the holidays, I was getting ready to clear my desk to go home. The bell had just rung for the dismissal of the children and in walked Gary with a GREAT BIG box with a BIG BEAUTIFUL red bow on it. I asked him if he wanted me to open it then - because there were teachers coming to check their mailboxes and the office was humming with its usual after school madness. He said, "Yep." So I opened the box to find a gorgeous long Ranch Mink coat. I jumped up and down - put it on and hugged and squeezed him tightly. Just the day before I put a silly little Christmas card in his lunchbox with a saying like, "What will we get each other for Christmas this year?" The man on the card held a new tie and the gal had on a new mink. (I often put cards or little notes in Gary's lunchbox to let him know I was thinking of him and how much I love him.) But boy, did this one pay off! I couldn't believe it . But it just so happened, the rest of the year after his accident, Gary was very busy with overtime jobs and he wanted to show me how much he loved me. He said, " I thought this would be something you had maybe dreamed of and I didn't want to wait until you were too old to enjoy one!" Actually I had three dreams in my life, to have a mink coat, a convertible and to go to Hawaii. Gary made all of those dreams come true. What a guy!

LESSON 17

YOU'RE NEVER TOO OLD TO STRETCH AND GROW

TRUST IN THE LORD WITH ALL THINE HEART, AND LEAN NOT UNTO THINE OWN UNDERSTANDING. IN ALL THY WAYS ACKNOWLEDGE HIM, AND HE SHALL DIRECT THY PATHS. PROVERBS 3:5-6 (KJV)

I had worked at my job as assistant secretary at Jackson Elementary for five years. I enjoyed each day because it was never boring - working in the office where staff, parents, students, administrators and the outside public visited all through the day. I had to be flexible because of all of the "pleasant" interruptions that occur and SMILE even if I didn't feel like it. Besides doing the general paper work, I typed, recorded attendance, took lunch orders, answered the phone, typed for teachers, copied papers, counted money, counseled and was "nurse" on the days the nurse was not at Jackson. Phyllis Blythe was the principal's secretary after Mrs. Kaletha retired. Phyllis and I hit it off from the first day we met! She was quite a "funny" lady and brought out the humor in me. Our friendship became special right from the start. It was wonderful to be able to work with someone pleasant by my side. We worked hard, but had fun too! We also were shoulders for each other to cry on when those times were needed. We both enjoyed singing, especially together.

It became an annual tradition for us to sing a duet of "White Christmas" at our secretary's Christmas dinner. And if anyone retired from the secretary's association, we were asked to sing, "May the Good Lord Bless and Keep You." We laughed as we called ourselves the "B Sisters."

We did not realize that our teamwork would come to a close so soon though. In 1988 our School Corporation had what we called a principal's shuffle. We had five schools and the principals switched jobs. They felt a change would be good. Mr. Miller, who was at Jackson, went to Yost Elementary and Phyllis went with him. Even though we would not work together any longer - we knew the friendship we had would never die.

We were expecting Dr. Daniel Keilman to be our new principal at Jackson. Dr. Keilman had been principal at Bailly Elementary for about seventeen years. We were excited about his arrival. We needed another secretary in the office. I had NO intentions of becoming the head secretary. I was comfortable where I was. Dr. Keilman started the interviewing process. He told me he wanted me to sit in on the interviews with a panel of teachers to decide who I would feel comfortable working with. The applicants were all so competent and "right" for the job. At the close of a long week of interviews it was time to make a decision. We all expressed our views and weighed out the pros and cons of each person interviewed. At the close of the last day, Dr. Keilman closed the door of the conference room, stood at the end of the long conference table and lowered his fist to the table and said while looking to the other end of the table," Nancy, I want you for my secretary!" All eyes focused on me, waiting for my response. My mouth flew open. I was speechless. (That was real unusual for me.) I broke out in a cold sweat and just sat there. My first words were, I didn't apply for the job. I can't do bookkeeping, I'm terrible in Math. I couldn't manage the whole office. For each I CAN'T someone in the room came back with a positive solution. I then looked at my boss and said, "I'll have to pray about it." He smiled and said, "O.K., you have five minutes." So I went next door in his office and prayed; "Oh Lord, what a step to make - longer eight hour days, more responsibility. Am I ready for this?" I also told the people waiting for me that I needed to call Gary. I thought, well, he probably wouldn't like for me to work forty hours a week. My prayer then became, "Lord, I'm going to call my husband and if you want me to accept this opportunity - new challenge -let the answer come through him." So, I nervously dialed our home phone. After three rings Gary answered (I think I woke him from an after work nap). When I told him what Dr. Keilman had asked me to do, and had asked, "What do you want me to do?" He replied. "Well, it's up to you. I think you could do it. Is there more money involved?" (Typical husband question.) I had expected," No, I'd rather you not work more hours. You know you can barely add 2 + 2", and all sorts of answers like the ones I tried to use as I presented my case.

But I heard only encouragement and thoughts of "I'm with you, Honey. Whatever you decide is O.K." Good wishes came through the telephone lines. "O.K. Lord, I guess I'm ready for a spurt of growth, I've been where I'm at for several years and could use some stretching and challenging." So, I took a deep breath and went back into the room where six people eagerly waited my answer. I said, "Yes."

We needed someone to take my job as assistant secretary. One of the ladies who had interviewed for the full time secretary position was Kay Sopata, a parent at Jackson, very personable, active in PTO and the community, a whiz at computers, was our choice. Kay and I worked side by side, and helped each other as co-workers (partners in crime as we sometimes said). Our relationship has grown so much. We worked well together, balanced each other out - (sometimes she had to come to my rescue and help me balance the bookkeeping out!) But it has been a joy to have her as a special friend, someone always there in good and bad times. And that is so important in our daily lives at work.

It takes a team to run a school office. It was such a blessing to work with Christians. I am so thankful that my third boss during my career was Dr. Linda Rugg. You don't always have a friendship like we had when you also work for someone as their Administrative Assistant. Last, but not least, was Pam Holbrook. We had so much fun! We also sang as we worked. We worked so well together we could finish each other's sentences.

I truly was blessed to have the job I had.

LESSON 18

JESUS' SUFFERING SOMETIMES BECOMES EVIDENT IN OUR SUFFERING

PRAY WITHOUT CEASING. 1 THESSALONIANS 5:17 (KJV)

Around October, 1991, we received a phone call from Tennessee that my mother-in-law, Audrey, was diagnosed with cancer. Our holidays were not going to be the same at our traditional yearly celebration. Ma and Pop would not be able to be in Indiana for our family Christmas. As we get older and things such as this come in our lives, we realize time and circumstances truly change our lives.

As we gathered around the phones on Christmas Eve, we took turns saying hello to Ma while she was lying in her hospital bed. This dreaded disease had not hit our family before. Being four hundred miles away from our family made things worse. Gary's brother Dennis stayed with his parents during the Christmas week, and then Gary and I went to Jackson, Tennessee, to spend the week with Ma and Pop in the hospital. Ma was diagnosed with cancer of the liver and bone. Her doctor spoke to us and told us her prognosis was, "She MAY live until June." Gary's dad had already stayed day and night with Ma for several weeks. We decided he needed to go home and sleep in his bed one night. (He had been sleeping in a chair every night at the hospital). Pop was in his seventies, and very strong physically because he had taken very good care of himself. But he still needed some time away to take care of some business and also rest. We finally talked him into the fifty mile ride home. I reassured him Ma would be fine and nothing would happen while he was gone.

Fifteen minutes after the men left, Ma started bleeding continually. As soon as the nurses and I changed her bed, she began bleeding again. She was helpless. It was so hard to see her that way. She would apologize for us having to clean her up. The nurse came in and said they were going to wheel her downstairs to take some tests to see where the bleeding was coming from. The tests required a signature, because of the risks involved. There I was by myself. I had no way to reach Pop and Gary. I had to make a choice concerning someone else's life. After I signed the papers and they wheeled Ma in the middle of the night to a room behind closed doors, I went to a nearby chapel and prayed. "Please help us through this night, Lord. Give me the strength to help Ma in anyway I can, no matter what may come." The bleeding continued all through the night and into the early afternoon the next day. The doctors had to give her five units of blood. The next day the men came to the hospital. I had called and let Gary know Ma was not doing very well. When they arrived back at the hospital, the doctors had ordered some more tests. The three of us walked next to the gurney and Pop held Ma's hand. We said goodbye once again and sat in a nearby waiting room and waited for Ma. While we were waiting, I picked up a magazine. (It happened to be a Christian Women Today magazine). As I opened the magazine up, it fell to a page with the scripture story about the woman with the issue of blood and how she touched Christ's garment and with her faith the bleeding stopped. I cried. But within five minutes a doctor came to the door and told us they didn't know where the bleeding was coming from exactly, but it had just stopped. "Lord, you are so precious. You use your word and prayer in our lives in so many ways." Ma shared with me the next day how she felt about this awful experience she had just gone through. She said, "You know Nancy, when I thought of all the blood I had lost - I realized it was nothing compared to the blood Jesus shed on the cross for me."

Ma in her suffering still touched lives with her words of Christ's love for us.

As I write this chapter in March of 1993, I am sitting in Ma and Pop's living room in Tennessee. It's a year and two months after the time the doctor said that Ma only had six months to live. She has suffered a lot and is suffering even now as I write, but God has a reason for her lingering on. I cherish each moment I have to hold her hand, wipe her brow, watch her loving husband wait on her and share his love with her by serving her - a lesson to us that true love is in sacrifice.

LESSON 19

GOD HELPS US LET GO
IF WE LET HIM

TRAIN UP A CHILD IN THE WAY HE SHOULD GO AND, WHEN HE IS OLD, HE WILL NOT DEPART FROM IT.
PROVERBS 22:6 (KJV)

It is so hard to spend eighteen years teaching, training, loving, and sharing in our children's lives and then to let them spread their wings and fly. I think it seems easier for fathers to let the children go. A mom has a harder time. At least this mom did!

When I look back at all of the times the children sat on my lap and listened to a story, I can still see their little eyes wander the pages of the books.

As I remember their voices say, "Mom will you take me to practice? Mom, can I have another cookie? Mom, I love you," my ears ring with JOY!

When I remember our daughter's voice singing in the school choirs and saw her feet lightly glide across the floor to the beat of the tunes, I smiled with pride.

I can still see the proud look on Gary's face as our son held his first fishing pole, made a home run, or pinned his opponent in wrestling and I clapped with excitement!

But, I also felt the warm tears stream down my face as I felt the heartbreak of our children when they had "breaking up times" with their teenage sweethearts, which were many. On those nights, I heard them crying in their rooms. I often wondered how I could sit back and watch our children fall on their faces – make mistakes, pay consequences - have to learn the hard way. I wanted to put a band-aid on their problems - to be there when the times were SO rough.

But Lord, thank you for showing me I can be there and love them unconditionally. But, I can't live their lives. That's how they grow! That's how they learn to depend on someone - and my prayer, Lord, is that I can let them go and let that someone be YOU!

P.S. Besides - their Dad needs me NOW!

God Blessed Our Years Together
With So Much Love and Happiness

Twenty five years ago
our lives became as one -
The time has flown by quickly
as I think of all we've done.

There have been times of joy and sorrow
with each passing day
We've held each other - Through the Years
And many times we'd pray . . .

Lord bless us with a life
of Love and Happiness
To share what you have given us
And do our very best.

God blessed us with two children
A boy and then a girl
They are just what we ordered
The Greatest in the world.

It's hard to be a parent
To teach what's right and wrong,
But with God's word and guidance
We prayed to be kept strong.

We think of times we had together
A family of four
We've loved, we've laughed, we've grown each one -
To love each other more.

But then there comes a time in life
To think of certain things
Like - two things you give your children
"One is roots and the second is wings"

How soon they use those wings
to start their own new life,
And we take each other's hands again
as husband and as wife.

We thank our wonderful family and friends
who've been there by our side,
To make our lives a special time
And in our hearts' abide.

So today we look to the future - We hold each others' hand,
We look in each others' eyes -
We pray again, "Lord continue to bless us
with a life of love and happiness.
Help us to be there for one another everyday,

Help us to continue to be there for our children, family and
friends.
We want to be the best Grandparents we can be, and show
our grandchildren YOUR love.
We know without you Lord our marriage would not have been
so "SPECIAL".
We want to have you as the center of our marriage for many
years to come.

And we will continue to be the best "fishing buddies" in the
world!

Written by Nancy Lee - With Love for Gary - 25th Wedding
Anniversary, 1993

LESSON 20

GOD CHANGES "THINGS"
BUT GOD NEVER CHANGES

MANY ARE THE AFFLICTIONS OF THE RIGHTEOUS; BUT THE LORD DELIVERETH HIM OUT OF THEM ALL.
PSALMS 34:19 (KJV)

It is now the summer of 1993. It has been two years since I began this book on "Life's Little Lessons". I had intentions to finish before now, but several things in my life have happened that postponed my writing or caused me to procrastinate. There are situations that happen that are better left unsaid or shared at certain times in our lives. When the unexpected problems or opportunities do come our way, we are faced with coping or rejecting, loving unconditionally or judging. With God's help we make it through and live with the changes.

So many changes come each day.

Toward the end of school in May I made the comment several times, "I am going to finish my book this summer break if it's the last thing I do." But, I did not expect the kind of "break" I got. I was tired of procrastinating. Well, with the end of school came the end of my work term. On June 16th I was free! (For two months). Gary and I had bought a new boat in January, (Our trip to Hawaii for our 25th Anniversary was postponed to do that). It was something we could use together since we are avid fishermen and fishing buddies. When we looked at the boats at the Marina, Gary found the one he liked. Well, I proved my "gracefulness" by tripping over the front of the boat which was tied to a post. I landed flat on my nose on the concrete. I came out of that with just some minor injuries, but pangs of muscle aches for months. I told him I literally fell "head over heels" for our boat.

We had so many plans for this summer. We took our new toy to Wisconsin for our yearly silver bass run. We had started fishing on Saturdays at a reservoir by his brother Dennis' home. We had gone perch fishing on Lake Michigan in our new boat. But the "Biggie" for this summer was a planned dream vacation to Ely, Minnesota, for the BIG FISH! Gary had dreamed of going there for ten years. We started making plans in March with two other couples, our friends the Foxx's, to go to Ely on July 16th for a week of fishing and fun. But for some reason, change took place once again. Jo Howerton, a third grade teacher from Jackson and dear Christian friend of mine, and I go to lunch and plan an afternoon together every summer. July 8th was our scheduled engagement. We went to lunch at a nearby restaurant and enjoyed the laughter and fellowship. Jo has a beautiful English garden in her back yard and I was anxious to see it and have her pick some daisies for me. (my favorite flower). When I dropped her off at her house, we walked to her garden and then to my car. Before I reached my car we were walking down her beautiful sloping lawn. The next thing I remember, my left leg stepped in front of my right - turned at the knee and then I heard a BIG crunch. I collapsed to the ground. I don't know if the sandals I was wearing was the cause, (Gary seems to think so) but I KNEW my leg was broken. I didn't know how badly. It was 90 degrees and Jo was so worried. She asked if she could help me in to the air conditioned house. I just replied, "No, Jo it's broken. I can't move. Call Gary." Her neighbor came over to ask if she could help. I remember biting my left thumb (since I had no bullet handy) and holding on to the grass blades with my right hand. Jo's neighbor called the ambulance while Jo called Gary. I remember thinking how ridiculous I must look lying on the side of the hill, but the pain was too intense to really care. Gary and Dawn arrived and then the ambulance came. The twenty minutes wait seemed like an eternity. (But little did I know how much waiting was ahead of me.) The paramedics strapped me on a stretcher and carried me into the ambulance. Gary and Dawn followed in the truck. Darren was living in Lebanon, Indiana. All I can remember was how painful it was. But the first remark I made to Jo was, "Oh no! Gary's going to shoot me! Our trip!" The paramedic wanted to give me some "happy gas" to help ease the pain, or at least help me to be less aware of it, but I knew I couldn't use that medication because of it making my heart race. So they gave me some oxygen, but they could give me nothing for pain.

When we arrived at the emergency room at the hospital, the emergency room doctor ordered some x-rays and knew right away I needed to see an orthopedic doctor. My ankle was out of socket, but the emergency room doctor didn't want to do anything until the specialist arrived. I had to be taken twice to the x-ray department. They gave me only one shot for pain and they turned, twisted, and rearranged my leg and hip in several ways to try and get a good picture of the damage. (It would have felt better just to get a picture with a Kodak!) The accident happened at 3:40 p.m. and at 7:15 p.m. Dr. Malayter arrived to put my ankle back in place. He was very gentle - and he gave me a local shot in the ankle to help with the pain as he worked on it. I just looked up at him and said, "Doc, can you get me in shape by next Friday? Gary and I are suppose to leave for Ely, Minnesota, for our dream fishing trip." (Gary was by my side, holding my hand.) Dawn had called my parents and brother, and they were all in the Emergency waiting room. Dr. Malayter grinned, shook his head and said, "Well Nancy, you have a very serious injury. You have broken your ankle bone in half and two bones in your leg are also broken. (I thought, "I walk three miles a day, how could this happen?") He said, " I will need to operate in the morning. I'll probably need to put a plate and five screws on one side of your leg and three screws on the other side. " You can ride 14 hours to Minnesota in the truck, sit in a lawn chair on the side of the lake and fish. You might could go in a boat - but what will you do in the middle of the wilderness if you get a blood clot in your leg?" Tears began to come from my eyes, not so much because of the pain in my leg anymore, (which there still was plenty) but because of the hurt and disappointment that our dream trip could not be taken. (At least at this time.) I questioned right then, "Why, Lord? Gary will be so disappointed. He's been looking forward to this for months. Well, I can talk him into going by himself anyway. I have a week - things could change."

Everyone went home after I was admitted to the hospital and I settled into my room. But after thirty minutes passed, Pastor Al Marquez arrived with his Bible in hand. He has been with us through some trying times in the past few years, and his sweet spirit and words are always a comfort.

Surgery was scheduled for 10:00 the next morning. Again my family was by my side. It was so reassuring and wonderful to know they would be waiting for me in the hall as I was wheeled back to my room after the operation. While in the prep room before surgery I overheard a young man in the next bed tell the nurse that he didn't have any family or friends with him. I wanted so much to say to him, "I'll share some of mine with you." I realized once again how fortunate I had been all my life to have such loving family who cared for me. Many people do not have this support.

Gary kissed me goodbye as I went through the operating room doors. It's always scary when you are put to sleep to go through surgery. It seems you are so out of control. And, there's always a risk. But I prayed the prayer, "Lord, I'm in your hands."

The surgery took a little over an hour and I remained in the recovery room for an hour or more, and then was wheeled back to my home away from home. It was so good to look up and see the faces of my family as I returned to my bed. The next couple days were hospital routine. I was hooked to I.Vs , drank clear liquids, had my temperature and blood pressure taken every couple of hours (around the clock). My leg had to be elevated all of the time with ice packs around it. I started receiving cards, visits and flowers from family and friends. The surgery was on a Friday morning and the doctor said I probably would go home Sunday or Monday. I would need to learn how to walk on crutches before leaving the hospital. He left the impression it would probably be Monday. He said another doctor would redress my leg and dismiss me.

Saturday night a little lady in her nineties was brought onto the floor with her third broken leg in one year. I remembered her voice from when I spent the night after my father's knee replacement surgery a few months before. She would yell all through the night, " Help! Help me!" She called out her husband's name (her husband had passed away many years before.) So I did not get very much sleep that night. On Sunday morning after a "real" breakfast, the physical therapists came in to take me for my lesson in crutches 101. They tried to stand me up Saturday afternoon but I still was too weak and faint from the surgery. So it was off to the parallel bars and hallway to try my skills. I was pretty wobbly but figured by afternoon I would be surer on my foot! When they wheeled me back to my room, Gary was there waiting for me. About ten minutes later the doctor who was to see me that day came in, introduced himself and said, "Well Nancy, are you ready to go home today?" I thought, ready as I'll ever be!

It has been two weeks since surgery, the staples have been taken out of my leg, (The plate stays in for two years.) A permanent cast has been put on for at least another four or five weeks. I am supposed to start back on the job in two weeks, but we'll see. My main concern as is the same as the doctors; that everything heals o.k. and I'm able to walk without a limp.

So once again I've asked the question "Why? Why did this happen now?" I've spent a week of nights and mornings crying because of spoiling mine and Gary's summer! But, there is a reason for everything. The disappointment will pass - even though I said I'll probably hear about this one for the next twenty five years! If I prayed for patience I might understand this happening, but like a lot of things in life, we won't understand why. This is just one more opportunity to know "God chooses what we go through and we choose how we go through it!"

The support of my family and friends has been overwhelming. Besides my husband staying home from fishing to take care of me in the evenings, Dawn Lee had just moved back home a week before the accident happened and had just quit her daytime job as a beautician. She has been such a sweetie to help me when needed. My mom and dad have come to the rescue as usual. My neighbors, co-workers from Jackson, and church members have all rallied and brought our meals to us. The Brechners, Earharts, Dueys and Smurdons, four couples we share Bible study and prayer with in our Growth Group on Tuesday evenings, have truly been wonderful prayer partners. My Joytime buddy, Sharon Tarry came to the rescue with a wheelchair. And my special friend Patricia, whom I walked with daily and shared joys and heartaches, even came over to clean my bathroom! God is so good! And sometimes He allows the busyness in our lives to cease. The daily calendar and lists of to do's we check off seem not so important. So, I can sit around and feel sorry for myself as I did at the beginning, blame myself, and waste my time crying and pouting. Or, I can look at it as a time once again to "Be still and know that He is God."

This summer before my broken leg, I returned several times to "my beach" on Lake Michigan to enjoy its beauty and magnitude. Sometimes, a couple of my beach buddies, Judy Floyd and Kathy Erdelac would go with me. I don't know if it was the beach or the delicious twisty ice cream cone we would buy on the way home, we enjoyed the most!

The cover of this book, portrays the beauty and works of God I see when I go there to retreat. How can people question if there is a God? The grains of sand, the wild grass, miles and miles of water, and seagulls flying in the heavens above are evidence of His creation. WOW! GOD IS SO AWESOME !

Whenever I go to the beach, I take a walk along the lake. There is a channel which I come to and have to cross. The thought of change really comes to my mind when I do this because it has changed in appearance each time. Some days it is wide and runs into the lake, some days it is narrow and runs along side of the water. Some days it is clear, and other days it is very dirty. On one of my early morning retreats I came upon a lady, Barb Moeller, who used to be our neighbor years ago. Barb had retired at sixty-two from being a doctor's receptionist in Chesterton and moved to Georgia. It was so neat to catch up on our families. We stood on the beach and talked for thirty minutes. She told of her divorce and how her five children from her first husband, who passed away, had bought her a new car so she could travel around the country and visit with them all through the year. But Barb always returned to the Dunes every summer to "her beach." We shared joys and heartaches of years past. She asked me what I did while coming to the lake so much. I told her I was writing a book - LIFE'S LITTLE LESSONS, sharing how Christ strengthens me in my life. I pointed to the channel and explained how I was going to use it as an analogy on change. I said, "Boy, it is really "yukky" lately though - so much deeper and so dirty. I won't even walk through it like that." She said, "Oh, I do. I wonder why I can and you can't," and smiled.

Well, we parted and walked in opposite directions, me toward the channel and her the other way. Two ladies were walking behind me as I came to the wide - "yukky" channel. I hesitated as I had the two previous days, then I said, "Oh if Barb can go through it so can I." I took a step and sunk into that oily, brown and green muck - all the way up to my thighs! I thought I had landed in quick sand! I turned to see if anyone was watching because I was SO embarrassed. The two ladies behind me were just ready to enter the waters I was in! I grabbed onto the sandbar behind me and pulled myself up - went over to the lake and rinsed the muddy sand off of me. Not to my surprise, the ladies decided to turn and walk the other way. I proceeded to my beach chair and decided to call it a morning. But before I left, I saw Barb walking toward me and I went to her and said, "Barb I thought I would walk through the channel today - since you did." I told her what had happened. She laughed and said, "Well I guess I made it through a little bit easier because I have twenty years on you Nancy!" We both agreed that that was a good lesson too. I told her she gave me some material to be used and we went on our separate ways.

That is true, the older we get, the wiser we can become through experiences and change. And no matter how high the waters get - how rough the waves rock us - how dark the clouds become - JESUS IS THE ANSWER.

Romans 3:23 says. "For all have sinned and fall short of the glory of God."

Romans 6:23 says. "For the wages of sin is death, but the gift of God is eternal life through Jesus Christ our Lord."

If you have not accepted this gift and you do not have Jesus Christ as the anchor in your life, or the lighthouse to show you the way, please consider asking Him to be your special friend. All you need to do is acknowledge you are a sinner, believe, and put your trust in Him and say a prayer as simple as this:

"LORD JESUS, I ASK YOU TO FORGIVE MY SINS, COME INTO MY HEART AND I WILL ACCEPT YOU AS MY PERSONAL SAVIOUR TO LIVE IN ME FOREVER. IN JESUS NAME I PRAY.   AMEN."

LESSON 21

COPING IN THE HARD TIMES

THESE THINGS I HAVE SPOKEN TO YOU, THAT IN ME YOU MAY HAVE PEACE. JOHN 16:33.

Gary's mother went to be with the Lord on May 27th, 1993. Her suffering ended as she rested in the arms of Jesus. Gary's father, Pop, moved back to Indiana to be close to his sons. He also had cancer. He had the disease while taking care of Ma, but unselfishly sacrificed and took care of her needs. We only had Pop with us a short time in Indiana. We spent a wonderful Christmas together in 1993, even though we missed Ma so much.

In April of 1994 I went to take care of my sweet father-in-law for the last nine days of his life. He taught me so much during his suffering. It was so hard to watch his health fail each day, but I saw his love for Jesus shine brighter each passing moment. As his three sons and I held his hands in his home in the early morning hour his last word was "PEACE".

God gave me the strength to sing "When Love Comes Home" at his funeral.

I often think of the words "Whatever Lord" from one of Barbara Johnson's book's - Splashes of Joy in the Cesspools of Life. Her book tells how she coped and managed to get through some real tragic life experiences. She shared how she gave everything to the Lord and let Him be in control.

During a short period of time Gary and I went through several challenges in our lives. After he lost his Mother, Father, an Uncle and two Aunts we both had to go through two surgeries. Both of our children got married in one year, and then they both experienced divorces. The job Gary was in charge of was losing money (which he had never experienced before). So many stressful things at once. One day I was at work and got a phone call from Gary. He was crying, very distraught. He told me I needed to come home, he didn't know what was happening to him. I quickly went to our school counselors' office and told him what was happening. Rick told me it sounded like he was having a nervous breakdown.

When I arrived home, I found my strong, in control husband, laying in a fetal position on the couch. I didn't know what to do. He did mention he knew how his best friend felt when he committed suicide just a few months before. I knew I had to get help right away.

We started seeing a Psychiatrist who put him on medication for depression. The doctor we saw was not a Christian. But through the medicine, resting and prayers of our Christian friends, Gary went back to work after six weeks.

During this time of depression, Gary spent many hours sleeping. I would go into the other room to pray and read a book I had previously bought, but not yet read. The book was by Carol Kent, titled "Tame Your Fears." As I highlighted the book, so many phrases and verses helped me get through each day.

My two friends, Patricia and Sharon were planning to go to Branson, Missouri to the Christian Women's Club Conference in June. It was a week long, wonderful time in the mountains to fellowship, learn and come closer to the Lord. I wanted to go, but I was afraid to leave Gary. I was drained, actually at the end of my rope. He encouraged me to go. He knew I needed a "pick me up", after all we had been through. I received a registration form in the mail and noticed who was the special speaker for the week. Yes, Carol Kent. I thought, how God's timing is so wonderful and unbelievable at times.

I decided to go. Little did I know what a healing time it was going to be.

Everywhere I turned, there were reminders of people and events that had just happened in my life. Gary's father, Pop, was a wonderful violinist. I used to play the piano for him when he played solos. I missed him and those times so much.

The first night began at the conference with a girl playing the violin. She played one of my favorite pieces Pop played. The tears began to roll down my cheeks. The message that Carol gave that night was the start of a week long journey through the scriptures and reminders of some of the hurts I had experienced. I thought I had gone to this conference to be happy. To heal. But I was feeling more sad as the days went on. "Lord, I could have stayed home and been sad."

The next day I went to a workshop presented by a dress designer. She created a wedding dress right before our eyes. Each piece of the dress represented a fruit of the spirit we should have in our lives.   When the dress was completed it was just like my daughter's wedding gown, right down to the pearls cascading down the back. I ran from the room in tears.

After three days of tears and questions, I realized something had to change. Before I went to bed on a Wednesday evening I prayed, "Lord, please put the JOY back in my life." Take my fears away. Sit on the throne of my life again.

About three o'clock in the morning I woke up from a terrible nightmare. I was in the same bed as Sharon and she saw me raise up in my sleep, like I was trying to attack something. Patricia was in the restroom, having a "feeling" that something was not right in our room. An eerie feeling. This may sound strange, but it is how it happened. I then relaxed and laid back down with a feeling of peace.

At seven o'clock in the morning I woke up with a song in my mind. With a tune on my lips, humming as I wrote the words. I opened the curtains and looked out over the mountains into a lake. I realized there was a battle going on in me the night before. I had prayed for JOY and Satan didn't want that in my life. But Jesus Christ won the battle. He gave me a song.

You Are There

When I look out over the mountains, You are there.
When I look into the waters, You are there.
When I think of all the strife, pain and tears in my life.
Lord you whisper, peace be still, I am there .

In the beauty of the flowers, You are there.
In the glow of the sunshine, You are there.
Sometimes doubt and fears may come, Disappointments, one
by one,
Lord you whisper, peace be still, I am there.

Teach me Lord to live by faith, You are there.
Give me hope, give me strength, You are there.
Put the JOY back in my life. Take away all foolish pride.
Lord you whisper, peace be still, I am there.

The next morning I had an opportunity to talk to Carol
Kent personally and tell her what had been happening in
Gary's and my life. She helped me so much, as she has
helped so many through her writing and speaking ministry.

I was asked to share my song at the conference as a
testimony for Christ.

It is so amazing how God can take our sad and trying
times and turn them into JOYFUL mountaintop experiences,
bringing us out of the valleys.

LESSON 22

SOMETIMES – WE JUST DON'T UNDERSTAND

DO NOT BE ANXIOUS ABOUT ANYTHING, BUT IN
EVERYTHING, BY PRAYER AND PETITION WITH
THANKSGIVING, PRESENT YOUR REQUESTS TO GOD.
PHILIPPIANS 4:6 (NIV)

"Why Lord?" That is a question we sometimes ask.
We should not question God. I have known that all of my life.
But in our humanness, it happens.

It was time for Gary to retire from working hard as an
Electrician for forty years. I was going to work at the school
until I was sixty-two. That was our plan. After Gary retired he
found himself missing the guys at work. He had worked with
his best friend, Larry, for all of those years. He started feeling
sad. He had noticed the last few years of his career he did not
have the confidence to run jobs anymore. He felt like being in
the background. But we weren't expecting another time of
depression. This time it was worse.

Gary had been a smoker for forty years. I prayed daily
that he would quit. He told me one day, when he retired, he
would. The second hand smoke all of the years he smoked,
definitely affected my asthma and breathing problems. Also,
affecting his health. I wanted us to have many more years
together. So with medication and a strong desire to quit, he
did. I was so proud of him. It was shortly after this time, he
started having symptoms of anxiety and depression. We
knew the signs. I once again sought out help.

When a person is in depression, it is hard for them to
make decisions. Even to know where they are headed. The
caregiver can recognize the symptoms sometimes when the
depressed person cannot. A lot of times the hurting one is in
denial. But Gary knew where he was headed. We started
going to a psychologist who dispensed medication. When you
are hurting and needing help, you rely on others advise and
care.

Many of our Christian friends started praying for Gary. We didn't keep it a secret that he was having a problem again because we knew the power of God and praying people.

The time kept dragging on. I was trying to keep working, but it was getting too hard emotionally to leave Gary alone. At one time he was on five antidepressants. He was like a zombie. It was very scary. He slept all of the time, he didn't want to see people. Except it was very strange. He has been an usher at church for many years. He loves serving in that position. Even during this time he would go on Sunday mornings, smile, greet people at the door. He would take up the offering. Then after the service he would walk to the car, and that was it. No conversations, no smiling. He would crawl back into his shell.

I was trying to give him some independence by allowing him to drive the car. But after almost two accidents, I wondered if I was doing the right thing. I finally decided, after another comment he made concerning being suicidal, I needed to retire.

I didn't wait until the end of the school year. I retired in January. It was so wonderful to work for people who were understanding and supportive. I knew I would miss the children and staff at school, but my first priority was to take care of my husband.

There was another problem though. Our insurance was running out for this type of medical care. I felt so anxious myself. I kept praying for strength and wisdom. I knew I had to hold it together for both of us. One night I was in tears and called our Senior Pastor, Bob Nienhuis. He was new to our church and I really didn't know him. But I was desperate. I told him the situation we were in. He suggested a Christian counselor. But our insurance did not cover him. He also suggested calling our Care Pastor, Cort Bucher, about a new program our church had just started. New Hope Biblical Counseling. And it was free.

Gary, through the help of Cindy Miller, the Director of New Hope and his counselor, David Beckwith, spent the next year, every week opening himself up to God's healing of Depression. He will testify today how God had to change his self-centeredness. He was always a perfectionist, a person in control at work and at home. But until he studied the scriptures, opened his heart and eyes to what the Lord had for his life in the future, God could change him into the man he is today. The scripture he memorized and relied on during this time was Philippians 4:6-7.

We also found a doctor who prescribed the correct amount of medication and helped Gary on the road to recovery.

This was another dark, lonely time in our lives. There is so much stress, worry, anxiety and depression in our world today. Again, Jesus is the answer! Not self. Not using the wrong kind of drugs. Not burying your problems and sorrows.

I had asked the question "why?" Now, I know the answer. We had to go in the valley to come out again on the other side, for Gary to come to the point where he is now, a counselor in the New Hope Counseling Ministry. People need people who have been there, who can identify with their problems. We give God the glory for bringing us to this point.

LESSON 23

HEAVEN AWAITS -
FOR THOSE WHO BELIEVE

BUT THANKS BE TO GOD, WHO GIVES US THE VICTORY THROUGH OUR LORD JESUS CHRIST. 1 CORINTHIANS 15:57

I was so blessed to have the most wonderful parents in the world. Dedicated to giving their lives and time to the Lord's ministry for sixty years.

As I mentioned at the beginning of the book, Dad was a preacher. A wonderful preacher that was not afraid to preach the gospel. He knew what the worldly life had to offer. He experienced it before becoming a Christian. He was a night club singer, golden glove boxer, living a life for the "devil". Then he met a little southern Christian girl, who would not marry him until he met her Savior. After he became a Christian they started on a journey together ministering in several churches. They were a "team", side by side through years of starting churches, building churches, and sharing the love of Christ to everyone they met. Dad was a bi-vocational pastor. He also built seventeen churches in Northwest Indiana. I could tell many stories of how the Lord used them during their ministry. But they always gave God the glory. They both have left a legacy that is a desire of my heart. Hopefully, someday my family and friends will remember me as a soldier for the Lord.

In my Mother's latter years she suffered from Parkinson's and dementia. She had to live out her last days in a nursing home because of a broken back. It was so hard to see her suffer, but knowing she knew her Savior was waiting for her in heaven gave her a peace through it all. She lived to be eighty six.

I had the privilege to have Dad live with us the last year of his life. He had congestive heart failure, and we had Hospice come into our home to help with his needs. They are angels here on earth. Another angel who was by my side when Dad passed away was my friend, Lorie Skimehorn. She came over when we knew my father only had a few hours to live. She is a Nurse, and knew the signs of death. She sent Gary and I to bed at ten o'clock p.m. and told me she would come get me when the time was near. She knew I had taken care of Dad until then and didn't want me to have to go through the final physical stages of cleaning him up and dealing with things I had never experienced before. At two thirty in the morning, she came to our door and said, "Nan, it's time." She was right. It was only twenty-five minutes later that he took his last breath and went to his home in heaven. It is amazing how God uses people in our lives just at the right time, people who have the gift of sacrificial serving and giving.

Dad did not want to stop ministering until he went to be with the Lord. One of his favorite persons in the Bible was Apostle Paul. He also wanted to run the race and finish the course! And that he did. I took him to the nursing home to give lunch devotions, sing and visit with people, three times a week. The funeral director asked me when we made arrangements for his funeral. "When did your Dad retire?" I said, "last Thursday." He passed away on the following Wednesday. He was ninety-three.

I was so blessed to have those kinds of role models in my life. To live here on earth for the Lord, knowing "Heaven Awaits- for those who believe."

Heaven also welcomed Gary's youngest brother, Craig and his wife, Leisa when they were killed instantly in a motorcycle accident in 2012.

Craig and Leisa were considered free spirits by their motorcycle club members. They were Harley people. Craig had been involved with alcohol and drugs for several years but he always had a sweet spirit. When he was younger he accepted Christ as his personal Savior. He went to a Bible college, and planned to serve the Lord. But then he chose a different path for his life. Even though he held down a job counseling people, he still used alcohol and drugs.

Then a friend encouraged him to join "Survivors – Clean and Sober." He became eleven years clean. Craig was offered a job as an assistant Warden at a prison. His new boss was a Christian. When he first started his job he had to stay in a Bed and Breakfast for awhile. The owner, a lady

(Grace), said if he stayed there she wanted him to go to church with her. Craig went to the Bible believing church. Leisa joined him in their new location. Their lives started to change. The Lord was really working. And they knew what was happening. They were so happy with all of the changes.

Craig and Leisa had ten children between them. They were grandparents.

Then in an instant, returning from a thirteenth anniversary celebration on Craig's motorcycle, they were both gone.

The witness that Craig and Leisa left from their last months of life was unbelievable. So many people gave testimonies at their memorial service. We miss them so much, but God was ready for Craig and Leisa to come home to heaven.

The desire of my heart is for people here on earth to know you can have a home in heaven with Jesus Christ after you leave this earth. Believing in Him and asking Him to live in your heart is the way.

These are the poems I wrote for my mother and father's funerals:

An Angel Here On Earth

There are Angels on this earth sent from God above-
To take care of His people and shower them with Love.
My Mother is God's Angel who had a rich, full life,
she was a perfect role model, as a Mother and a wife.

When Mom was just seven, her mother passed away,
Before my Grandmother closed her eyes she had these words to say.
Please promise me Juanita - be a good girl and marry a "Christian" man.

My Mother kept her promise as she held her Savior's hand.
My Mother found that special man -
But God's love he did not know,
She shared Christ with this man she loved,
remembering the promise she made years ago.

God called these special people into the ministry -
A life of love and sacrifice, a life so blessed and free.
As Mom stood by my Father's side, for a wonderful sixty five years,
They have shared and prayed and cared for others through laughter and through tears.

You may have heard my Mother teach God's word with all of her heart, or watched her play the piano, she always did her part.
God used her as a leader, a prayer warrior, a friend.
Such faith and trust in Jesus, she had until the end.

Our family has sweet memories of my Mother's precious smile.
All of our great traditions that she started with such style.
Her grandchildren call her blessed, and their children see that too,
her wisdom and example will help show them what to do.

Mom has had a lot of suffering and pain -
but I know within my heart she believed "For to me to live is Christ and to die is gain."
I may cry because I'll miss her, this precious Mother of mine.
But I will weep with Joy in my heart, because she's with her Savior divine.

In Loving Memory
Nancy Lee

A Precious Man Of God

This man, we are here to honor today,
has a special place in my heart.
He is my Father, a spiritual leader,
who truly gave me a great start.

We have all heard his life story,
of the days he was quite wild.
But we know when he met my Mother,
his ways changed, to become more mild.

Her quiet, loving spirit,
came from her Savior above.
She knew Jesus Christ was the only answer,
for them to have true love.

I know there were many sacrifices
this man made to help people -
It was part of his daily life,
not just on Sunday under a steeple.

God gave him many talents,
a voice to sing beautiful songs.
A desire to build churches,
a place for Christians to belong.

In his latter years, he wasn't ready to quit.
He walked nursing home halls
with a smile on his face,
and a greeting with quick wit.

One of his dreams, goals, or desires in life,
was to show Christ's love on his face,
like Paul in the Holy Bible -
He ran the course and finished the race.

A race that was well worth the journey,
down the many roads he had trod.
A wonderful legacy he has left us -
This precious man of God.

In Loving Memory
Nancy Lee

LESSON 24

THE JOY OF GRANDCHILDREN

CHILDREN'S CHILDREN ARE A CROWN TO THE AGED, AND PARENTS ARE THE PRIDE OF THEIR CHILDREN. PROVERBS 17: 6

It is such a blessing to be Grandparents! I was a young "Nana". The only one of my friends who had grandchildren. So I was always pulling the brag book out of my purse to show my three older granddaughter's pictures. I started feeling that my friends were getting bored with my "showing off." Until they all started having grandkids. Then they realized the feeling. There is nothing like it! You are always proud of your own children when they are growing up. But then when your children have children –WOW, it is such a different feeling. I guess you are so proud of what your children have given you.

Darren gave us four wonderful girls. Dawn and Chago gave us an awesome boy and girl. The thrill of seeing your children parenting also warms your heart. You may see mistakes that they make in raising their children, but it is a time in your life that you pray and "zip up your lips." You think back over your life and realize some of the choices you had made when you were younger were not good ones. Then you had children. They didn't always make the right decisions and had to pay the consequences. There are two things parents give their children. Roots, and then wings to go out on their own. It is so hard to let go. It is even harder at times having adult children, To know when to give advice and when to keep quiet and pray. We have always tried to not interfere in our children's lives. They know we are here and when they come to us for advise we are always there for them. Through the years it has been so wonderful to get cards from our son and daughter sharing how much they love us and how much we have helped them. Too many times parents try to live their children's lives for them. It doesn't work that way. We have gone through a lot of hurts and tears in our family because of choices that may not have been the best. But unconditional love has been the key to staying close together through these times.

Now, our grandchildren are growing up so fast. The old saying, " enjoy them while they are little, they grow up right before your eyes", is so true. I had always heard also, "they step on your feet when they are little, and on your heart when they are big." I don't think that is intentional in our case. But challenges do come into everyone's family.

When our six grandchildren were babies I gave them nicknames. The oldest, Erailia Marie was Angel. Rachel Renee' was Punky-doodle. Samantha Lynn was Cuddle-bug. Payton Drew was Mr. Magoo. He could not say Mr. Magoo, he said Mr. Doody. So that became his pet name. Karissa LeeAnne was Princess. Jaida Brie was Sweet Pea. They didn't always like those names, but they tolerated Nana calling them by their "silly" names at times. Now that they are ranging from twenty-one down to eight, I still call them by those names. I try not to embarrass them in public. Well, I don't always stick by that rule!

When the grandchildren come over we always give them a hug. I am one who wears lipstick all of the time. My kisses on the cheek or forehead became a "Nana mark." Sometimes they would run from me, or say ,"did you give me a Nana mark?"

I enjoy this time in my life. Going to Grandparent's Day, concerts, ball games. I have a Nana Camp every summer. We do all kinds of fun things together. Go to the beach, crafts, share stories, play dress up, have a snack shop. Every year is different. Even the older ones wish that time in their life didn't end. Life is full of negative things if you look for them. But life can have happiness and fulfillment if you concentrate on the positive. It is not the material things you give your children and grandchildren that makes happiness. It is the time you give them and the love you show them through Jesus Christ.

This is an article I had printed in our local newspaper:

Everyday we see, hear, or read about negative things young people do in our world. We need to tell the positive actions of our teens, when they happen. I would like to share a story about an eighteen year old young lady who saw a situation, and gave of herself in a very compassionate manner.

Samantha was traveling on a country road near her home in Moss Bluff, Louisiana on a late, dark, night after work last month. She came upon an accident where the car was on fire. Sam got out of her car, walked toward the scene and called 911. She then noticed a person lying on the ground on the road. He was the driver of the car. There also was one passenger that she was not aware of at the time. Samantha sat down next to this twenty five year old man, held his hand and assured him he was not alone, and he was going to be ok. Jerry had a wife and a six year old son. Sam stayed until help came. Jerry and his passenger were taken to the hospital. The passenger was in a coma. Jerry passed away.

I am so thankful for the courage, compassion and Good Samaritan act of my granddaughter, Samantha Lynn Beavers (previous Chesterton resident). She since then has decorated a cross and taken flowers to the site where the accident took place. Jerry was a stranger to Samantha, but that didn't matter to her, she proved to be "An Angel here on earth."

Sam's compassion helped Jerry's family know he was not alone, and my heart was touched in a very special way.

I would also like to share an essay that Payton, fourteen, wrote for school. It brought tears to my eyes.

MY GRANDMA

My grandma Nancy, also known as Nana by us grandkids, is the best grandma that I could ever have. She lives in Chesterton, Indiana, and we visit her every year on all of the holidays and other occasions such as birthdays and more. She always mails things to us and I am always happy when she does. I am her only grandson so she always takes me places and helps me with homework when I see her.

My grandma has gray hair that she dyes black because she doesn't like to look old. She wears glasses and always wears gym shoes, even in the house because she has very

weak feet and they hurt her. She always forgets things and I
have to remind her sometimes. My grandpa and I tease her
and say that she is losing her mind.

When I was really little I used to go to her house every
weekend and play games and go to church with them. She
always used to give me candy and let me color so I would be
quiet during church. Every summer my three cousins and I
would go to her house for a week for Nana Camp where we
would make Nana Camp shirts, do crafts, and go to a lot of
parks. My three big cousins are in their twenties and late
teens so they don't go to Nana Camp anymore. My sister,
little cousin and me are the only ones who go now.

She has recently been doing many things that she has
always wanted to do. She has been parasailing, zip lining,
and many more things. Last month she visited Greece with
her church group for a week. She had an awesome time and
she took a lot of pictures. But, when she was walking up a
mountain one day, she stepped in a hole and broke her foot.
Some of the guys in their group had to carry her back down
the mountain, with one person on her left, one person on her
right, and one person in the back.

My grandma is probably one of the funniest people I
know. She always knows how to make people laugh, even
when they are in a bad mood or sad. Her and my grandpa got
a Husky last year and named it Koda. She is really hyper so
my grandma has to watch her foot when Koda is around,

Even though my great grandpa James Mills passed
away about two years ago she has been mostly the same
person, I think that when my great grandpa passed away she
had a hole in her heart; so she bought Koda. Koda filled my
grandma's heart and has loved her. She still misses him and
talks about him a lot, but I can see that she has moved on and
focused on her children and grandchildren.

My grandma has taught me that you should have as
much fun as you can when you are young because when you
get older you will realize you're too old to do anything fun. I
will always remember my grandma and she will always
remember me too.

That's why I enjoy being a Nana!

I have been a Mentor for MOPS (Mothers of Preschoolers) at our church for the past few years. It is a wonderful international organization for moms to get together twice a month. A time to share ideas, problems, listen to speakers on parenting. I wish MOPS was around when I was a young mother. Young married people need each other and help to guide them in parenting their little ones.

Children are the future. We as the older generation can help guide them in the right path. And the best path in life is following Jesus Christ.

LESSON 25

CELEBRATE EVERYDAY
THIS IS THE DAY THE LORD HAS MADE,
LET US REJOICE AND BE GLAD IN IT. PSALM 118:24

I am known as adventuresome. Especially since I am older and filling out my "bucket list." I guess that is a way to say, doing things I've never done, before I leave this old earth! In the past few years I have gone parasailing. That was quite a stretch, since I am not a swimmer and I went 400 feet above Lake Erie. I made the young men in the boat promise me they would set me down in the boat and not in the water.

I have wanted to zip line. So last summer I found out one of our friends have a zip line in their backyard. It is not a big one, but none the less, a zip line. I did that. It took me fifteen minutes to push off of the perch, but I made it. When I tell people I've been zip lining, they don't have to know how far!

I have always wanted to go overseas to another country. So Gary and I went on a trip to Greece and Turkey with twenty-six wonderful people from our church. It was so well planned by our pastor and the tour guides. It is a good thing Gary and I didn't go out on our own. For more reasons than one!

The trip was for ten days. An exciting, rigorous schedule. It was an opportunity to go on Paul's Second Missionary Journey. We visited the ruins in Thessaloniki.

Our tour guide, Costas was a wonderful Christian Greek man who shared not only the culture of the cities, but the Biblical aspect of everything we saw. It was such a wonderful feeling to see and know we were walking where Paul once walked.

There was a young man with our tour group who was from Greece. His name is Theo. We became close in just a few days. He is an amazing young man. A Lawyer, a preacher, a leader who has a heart for the people of his country. His desire is to spread God's word in any way he can. We plan to keep in touch with Theo. He has made many sacrifices to help his family. The world needs more men like Theo.

We spent a few days in Athens. We shopped at the markets. So many things to see. We went to the Acropolis. My goal was to go to the top and stand on Mars Hill where Paul gave his sermon in Acts, and where my father preached in 1967. It was a tough trip up the mountain because of having a brace on my bad right knee. But I made it. It was a wonderful time to celebrate! I cried tears of joy, as I felt the blessings of God, and knowing my Dad spent some time there.

Gary helped me down the mountain. Then it happened! Yes, once again another broken bone. It always has something to do with trips. We were about fifty feet from the gate on a brick sidewalk. I found a big hole in the sidewalk. But too late! I fell to the ground with a broken ankle.

Everyone came to my rescue. Our pastor's wife Bette Jo is a Nurse. Katie, a young gal in our group is a Physical Therapist. And Rick, who went and got a wheelchair, is an Anesthesiologist. I tried to keep a sense of humor, and told Rick to "just put me under." Several people had prayer for me before we called for an Athen's taxi to go to a hospital. Oh my, you have never had a ride, until you've been in Athens, Greece in a taxi.

With the help of Costas, our tour guide, and George Romeos, our missionary in Greece I received great care. I was concerned about being in a foreign country, especially since the day before this happened I went on Medicare. My sixty-fifth birthday would be in two days. I could see dollar signs! But God helped us with this too. I was at a small, private hospital. I had an x-ray. I saw an Orthopedic doctor. She put a plaster cast on my ankle. All for two hundred Euros. That is $273.36 in American currency. It would have cost us thousands of dollars back home.

We still had five days left of our trip. I could have called it quits. But Gary and I figured we would never be in Greece again. The doctor said to keep my leg elevated. Well, that is kind of hard on a trip like we had planned. I did stay in bed at the hotel the next day while the group went to Corinth.

Our plan was to go that evening to the CosmoVision Center where George and Marcy Romeos have their ministry. Foutis, George's brother is also a leader in this organization. George drove sixteen miles through Athens traffic to come and get me for dinner with the others. Everyone just went out of their way to help me finish the trip. I don't know how people live without the Lord and Christian friends.

The CosmoVision Center is a wonderful outreach to countries all over the world. They have many departments aiding all types of needs. We could see the heart of the ministry through the words and humbleness of those who lead it.

I had another chance to practice my life's verse. "I can do all things through Christ who strengthens me." Philippians 4:13. We went on a two hour tour through the cobblestone streets of Ephesus. Another amazing area where Paul ministered. Two young Greek men from the tour company joined us and pushed the wheelchair (along with Gary and some other men from our group) so I could finish the tour. God is so good!

We also were on a cruise ship for three days. It was not very wheelchair accessible, but we managed. The view of the islands was breathtaking. We had never been on a cruise before. The food and service was great! I even got to celebrate my birthday with some people from our group with a complimentary birthday cake.

The last day was a Sunday and we had a worship service on the ship. There is something beautiful about sharing testimonies and singing God's praises together. "Great is Thy Faithfulness" is one of the songs we sang.

Our last stop was the awesome island of Santorini. I looked at the tender boat that we had to get on to get over to the island. I was in a wheelchair and not a swimmer. Could I do it? Sure, why not? So the guys on the boat helped me get onto the boat. We did not go to the top village on the island, but enjoyed watching the sunset on the lower level. The rest of the group took a cable car to see the main part of the island.

The trip was truly a time of celebration with my wonderful husband and friends. A memory for us to share for the rest of our lives.

The greatest JOY I had on this trip was seeing Gary reach out to people from all over the world. He was always the first one to greet people in the elevators. He would ask them where they were from. If he could not speak their language, he would use the translator on his phone to talk to them. This was another time I could see how God had changed Gary's life. His openness to share Christ's love with others.

Celebrating life doesn't have to be doing adventuresome things. It could be taking a walk on the beach. Looking at the colors of Fall. Feeling snowflakes fall on your face. Watching new growth when Spring arrives.

Celebrate each day, what God did for you through His Son.

The LESSONS you can learn from JESUS are precious and priceless.
Please write to me and share the JOY of your decision or LESSONS you've learned from God.

Write to: Nancy Lee Beavers
904 N. 100 West
Chesterton, IN 46304
nancylbeavers@comcast.net

Made in the USA
Charleston, SC
19 March 2015